THIS BOOK BELONGS TO:

....

T0243624

A
BOOK
THAT
LOVES
YOU

A

flow

BOOK

A
BOOK
THAT
LOVES
YOU

An Adventure in Self-Compassion

IRENE SMIT and **ASTRID VAN DER HULST**

Workman Publishing ✳ New York

Library of Congress Cataloging-in-Publication Data is available.
ISBN 978-1-5235-1319-2

Design by *Flow* magazine and Rae Ann Spitzenberger
Cover illustration by EurekartStudio
Additional art credits appear on page 216

Workman books are available at special discounts when purchased
in bulk for premiums and sales promotions as well as for fundraising
or educational use. Special editions or book excerpts can also be created
to specification. For details, contact the Special Sales Director at
specialmarkets@workman.com.

Workman Publishing Co., Inc.
225 Varick Street
New York, NY 10014-4381
workman.com

flowmagazine.com

Printed in China
First printing August 2022

10 9 8 7 6 5 4 3 2 1

CONTENTS

OPEN YOUR ARMS, TURN THE PAGE

If you're holding this in your hands, it likely means that you already know how special books are. You know that they have the power to uplift and affirm, to offer escape and bring comfort. We love books, but can books love us back?

We believe they can: Through their text, their stories' characters, and even the tactile experience of turning a page, books can offer solace, words of advice, and support when we need them most. A book can be a trusted friend and wise confidante by offering commiseration, alternative perspectives, or an escape. And like good friends, books nourish and take care of us, understand us, inspire us, and make us *feel*.

We started our magazine, *Flow*, more than a decade ago in the Netherlands, our small corner of the world, to let our readers know: *We see you*. We see you, because we are you. We often feel like you do. Sometimes overwhelmed by life. Sometimes insecure and anxious about all the changes happening around us. We understand how daunting it feels to get out of bed every morning when energy reserves are depleted. We know how it feels to have asked too much of oneself on any given day. We know what it feels like to live with stress, because we do. And we know how it feels to look in the mirror and feel less-than because we are not living up to our own or society's unwieldy standards. We know how it feels to be alone or under-appreciated. And we know how freeing it can feel to be able to show up regardless, as you are, perfectly imperfect. Because we also know how beautiful life feels when we are able to focus on the tiny pleasures that exist in the spaces and experiences around us. When we can focus our attention and really recognize the things around and within us that make life special, it opens us up to more understanding and acceptance. We feel better equipped to surf the sometimes unforgiving waves of life, to laugh more when we fall in, and to let get go of the fear of awkwardly climbing back up. In other words, we are better at taking life as it is and as it comes.

If you're familiar with our magazine or our previous books, you also know that we have a fondness for paper that extends far beyond the limits of a flat, bound-in page that can be turned. We believe that interacting with paper can help us balance the bigger things in life. Which is why you'll find, nestled among these pages, joyful paper surprises like a nature sketchbook, a fill-in user's manual to help you and your loved ones get to know you better, a series of bookmarks, a collection of postcards, a sticker puzzle, and a punch-out-and-assemble flower to give yourself anytime—just because.

We hope that these activities, along with the articles and essays from *Flow*, will help you more easily navigate life. We already know these words, and their lessons—that we revisit again and again—have helped us. In the following chapters, you'll read about the advantages of anxiety and worry—and how to balance it; about loving your imperfect body (and recognize that we're all imperfect);

about being alone without feeling lonely; about finding comfort in ritual even amidst your ups and downs; about accepting your uniquely brilliant mind; about being okay sitting in idleness; and about our personal favorite: letting go.

Through this journey together creating *Flow* and translating the best parts of it into this book, we (Astrid and Irene), have learned to be less demanding of ourselves and better at moving along with life rather than against it— embracing the difficult stuff it throws at us and making room for failure. We've also each learned to appreciate some of the little things that make us who we are as individuals.

FOR IRENE, IT'S:

- My creative brain
- My thoughts, even though they scare me sometimes
- My ability to come up with solutions to difficult problems
- The way my blue eyes become more vibrant when the sun is shining very brightly
- My inner child that feels so lost now and then

FOR ASTRID, IT'S:

- The so-so days when I feel jealous of everyone on social media who appears to be doing nicer things
- My ability to adapt to new circumstances
- My overactive brain that is always filled with new plans
- My mood swings
- My intense love for open water that makes me brave enough to swim in the lake in winter.

What are some of the little things you acknowledge and celebrate about yourself? (Go ahead, give yourself some compliments!)

FOR ME, IT'S:

▶

....

....

▶

....

....

▶

....

....

▶

....

....

▶

....

....

We hope this book feels like a big warm hug to you—that it is a supportive, mindful companion in times when you need a boost. Whatever happens, whatever comes on your way, however often you are your own worst critic, remember that with every turn of its pages: *This book loves you … just the way you are.*

Irene & *Astrid*

Chapter 1

LOVE YOUR ACTIVE BRAIN

OH, THAT HEAD OF YOURS—THAT BRILLIANT, complex brain that never stops coming up with more things to think of. Do you ever go out for a walk to try to clear your head only to return with more new plans than you left with? Or maybe you take a shower in the evening to let the water wash away the day, then find yourself scribbling more new ideas in the notebook by your bed? Or, perhaps when you try to meditate, all kinds of things keep popping into your head.

It can be exhausting to have to address our own heads with a stern *Umm . . . excuse me, but can we have a bit of quiet up there?* It's especially the case when our thoughts are worry-based, and we can't seem to shake them. Whether they're about deadlines, relationships, new projects, or future exams, when it gets too crowded in our heads, we (Irene and Astrid) like to get together and have a little complaining session about all the activity up there. Until one of us says, "Hey, but we should be grateful for it. Isn't it great that our minds always come up with great ideas? With new solutions? With creative plans? With new options when we feel stuck?" The flipside of having a busy mind, of course, is that you can always trust it to come up with a new plan, a way forward, or a possible solution to a problem. It's your mind's way of looking after you. It is important to discover what allows you to relax, while allowing yourself the space to embrace your thoughts and your worries. Your overactive mind is one of the things that makes you *you*.

LET'S HEAR IT FOR THE WORRIER!

BY SARA MADOU

Some minds rarely take a rest—thoughts keep whirring, even through the night. But what if you could let worrying and mental rumination work to your advantage?

It had been a tough day at work. When I finally got to bed that night, almost everything I had said and done kept replaying in my mind. Should I have handled the meeting differently? And why didn't I call out that colleague about her unkind remark?

It's not unusual for me. When I'm in the middle of a brain-churn, I sometimes fantasize about having a panic button. Because even though I *know* that it doesn't help to think back on an awkward conversation I had ten years ago, I do it anyway. Sometimes I worry about why I'm worried about it. Or my mind jumps to big global issues such as climate change. A good friend said something a while ago that was a real eye-opener: "Overthinking is your strength. The hyperactive jumps you make in your head are great for coming up with creative ideas. Not just for your work, but also when other people have a problem they can't solve." Her kind words are food for thought: What if we let worrying work in our favor?

ACCORDING TO THE STOICS

"He who fears he shall suffer, already suffers what he fears" is a well-known quote attributed to French philosopher Michel de Montaigne. But the Stoic philosophers realized this as early as the third century BCE with the claim that feelings are the root of our thoughts: You feel anxiety because you think something will fail. You feel joy because you believe in your brand-new relationship. The problems arise if you stray too far in one direction.

We can tie ourselves in knots with our thoughts. In fact, whether what we're thinking is true or not, about 60 percent of our worrying concerns matters over which we have no influence—like what others think of us, or something that happened in the past.

The term rumination comes from the Latin *ruminare*, which means both to "chew the cud" and "to turn over in the mind"—both definitions indicate a process of finding a solution to a situation or problem, which can easily be understood as a positive.

ALWAYS A PLAN B

With a new perspective I have come to realize that my very busy head has helped me a lot. In my line of work it's important to be able to brainstorm, so having a mind that connects so many

Even though I know it doesn't help to think back on an awkward conversation I had ten years ago, I do it anyway.

different wires is very useful. The fact that I often think about every possible scenario is tiring, but also quite handy. For vacations, for example, I figure out exactly how to get to our rental house and research what to do in the area. And I always have a plan B (and C and D) ready, just in case.

Dutch communications expert Loes Vork can relate. "I've always had a head that just won't stop," she says. "But I get a lot out of it, too. Yes, I see problems everywhere, but that also means that I'm better at solving my clients' issues. It's only when I am tired or emotional that it's difficult—the negativity takes over."

Vork has had to teach herself to have a more positive view. "I've always had creative hobbies," she says. "I worried that my love for crafting contradicted my career. I now know the two can coexist. My communications clients love my creative brain—and I always carry a notebook with me as an outlet to write down all of my restless ideas. At home, I throw a cloth over the birdcage, as it were. My phone is switched off and I take up a crafty project that engages my hands rather than my head. Part of taking good care of yourself is viewing situations from different angles."

HEALTHY AND SMART

According to a study by psychology professors Kate Sweeny and Michael Dooley of the University of California, Riverside, worriers often have better health because, for example, they smoke less and are more conscientious about using sunscreen. "Worry also serves as an emotional buffer," they write, "by providing a desirable contrast to subsequent affective reactions." In other words, if you are concerned about something that might happen in the future, then you experience more positive emotions about what actually happens; if you worry about how terrible something can be, it's a big relief when it turns out to be less terrible. The researchers also discovered that worrying is motivating: Such thoughts work like a red flag—something is wrong!—so that you are spurred to act.

Another positive was discovered by assistant psychology professor Alexander Penney from MacEwan University in Canada: People who worry a lot are, on average, smarter. In his study, "Intelligence and emotional disorders: Is the worrying and ruminating mind a more intelligent mind?," he writes, "It is possible that more verbally intelligent individuals are able to consider past and future events in greater detail, leading to more intense rumination and worry." This theory is supported by evolution: Early humans that could recognize what threats they might run into had better chances of survival.

WHAT IF . . . ?

But worrying, of course, also has disadvantages. All the scenarios that occupy your thoughts prevent you from being in the present. As with most things, it's about striking a

THE UPSIDE OF WORRY

- You are better prepared for, and less upset by, unpleasant situations.

- You are more grateful when something goes well.

- You understand consequences.

- You have an eye for detail.

- You are thoughtful and plan ahead.

- You are reliable and good at setting priorities.

balance. When I share my thoughts with someone I trust, I can sometimes hear myself talking and become aware of the moment when my thoughts derail.

I've also become a fan of "defining your fears," as American entrepreneur and author Tim Ferriss calls it. In short, you write down what the worst thing is that could happen to you if you take certain steps, then focus on prevention. Next, write down what happens if your goal is successful, and what can happen if you choose not to do it. These steps came in very handy when I was considering quitting my job (and the security that came with it) and opting for a freelance life. As doom scenarios, for example, I wrote "an uncertain life" and "feeling lonely without colleagues." To prevent these things, I noted that I could look for regularly recurring freelance jobs and rent a workspace in an office with other freelancers. And by channeling my outcomes onto the page, I was able to structure them, and gain clarity on what to do.

DARE TO THINK

"Thinking deeply about something is essentially a positive thing, but we often suffer from our thoughts," says Maria Janssens, cofounder and head of content at The School of Life in Amsterdam. Worrying itself is not really the problem, but how we experience it is.

"Very special thoughts are created by worrying. The German philosopher Immanuel Kant was right when he said, 'Dare to think.'" Janssens continues, "Worrying is often a sign of love." Whether it is about the people around you, your reputation, your career, or something completely different, when you worry, you're showing that you care." We worry when we love, and love is and will always be one of the most beautiful things we have.

WANT TO READ MORE?

- *Meditations* by Marcus Aurelius

- *How to Stop Worrying and Start Living* by Dale Carnegie

- *My Friend Fear: Finding Magic in the Unknown* by Meera Lee Patel

live by
your own
MOTTO

Never give up on the things that make you smile.

TRUST the timing of your *life*.

It's important to remember that you are MAGIC.

Be BRAVE. Take RISKS. Nothing can substitute EXPERIENCE.

Collect pretty buttons in one or more
colors. Arrange them in a way that makes
you happy, and then draw them.

Empty all the items from your handbag,
arrange them in a line, and draw them.

**Glue a shopping list or receipt here and
draw the first five items on the list.**

**Cut out shapes from pretty pieces of paper and glue
them down like a garland across the bottom of the page.**

**Draw a tree. Find a pretty leaf outside
and stick it to your tree.**

**Cut out letters from a newspaper, arrange
them into a word, and stick them down.**

**In your best handwriting, print the
title of the first book you see.**

**Think of a favorite moment you spent on,
in, or by the water. Make a drawing of it.**

Cut out a little stack of circles from colored paper. Arrange them into a collage and glue them in place.

Cut out and glue one half of a photo from a magazine in this space, then draw the other half yourself.

LIFELONG LEARNING ABOUT OURSELVES

*We learn to live our lives through what we experience,
hear, and read. What have you learned about yourself and life?
What things could prompt you to make different choices now?*

WHAT WOULD YOU LIKE TO FIND OUT ABOUT YOURSELF?

WHAT IS YOUR MOST RECENTLY ACQUIRED LIFE LESSON?
WERE YOU READY FOR IT, OR DID IT COME AS A SURPRISE?

**WHO INSPIRES YOU TO GET TO KNOW YOURSELF
BETTER AND TO DISCOVER NEW THINGS?**

**WHAT ADVICE WOULD YOU SHARE
WITH YOUR FIFTEEN-YEAR-OLD SELF?**

LEARNING TO THINK

BY SJOUKJE VAN DE KOLK

At a time when you can google just about everything, it's easy to forget to think for yourself. Dutch philosopher Minke Tromp encourages us to exercise our mental muscle a bit more.

How Do You See the Times We Live In?

Today we are expected to be so driven and results-oriented that we forget to stop and think. I call it the success paradox: The more success you have, the less space you have to reflect, and the more trapped you become in your own ambition. But reflection actually becomes even *more* important when you're successful at what you do. This applies to people's work, but also to their private lives. We're hardly able to tell the difference anymore between the good feeling we get when we're doing well and the adrenaline that's just keeping us going, the latter actually draining us without us even being aware of it.

How Did This Happen?

Efficiency is seen as the most important thing in our time. We tend to constantly think in terms of goals and means: I have to do *this* to achieve *that*. And when things succeed, it only serves to confirm and amplify that form of goal-oriented thinking. This makes sense, because when we're on to a good thing we generally like to have more of it. The upshot is that results-driven thinking is growing. After all, we have achieved enormous successes over the past fifty years: We've put a human on the moon, we've witnessed a huge increase in general prosperity, and technology is developing at an incredibly rapid pace. Success makes us want more and that's how this way of thinking— targeting efficiency and speed—has gotten the upper hand.

So We're Trapped.

We are so enchanted by our own success that we often don't even really know why we do the things we do. This leads to a sense of dissatisfaction at the very least, and burnout in the worst case, but also to poor decision-making, which can eventually cause harm. My role is to get people to think more deeply by asking them *why* they are doing what they are doing. Often their first response is to question what good can come of thinking about it. This is a results-driven question. Only when I add a promise— for example, that they will feel happier or more

ALWAYS KEEP ASKING QUESTIONS INSTEAD OF Searching for ANSWERS

—MINKE TROMP—

purposeful or more satisfied—are people willing to think about the question. But these important questions often go unasked.

▸ How Can We Break the Pattern?

This might sound a bit convoluted, but the solution can be found in the thinking itself. Thinking has a bit of a bad reputation nowadays: We're supposed to feel more, and thinking is blamed for all sorts of problems. But thinking is far more than the stream of thoughts that pass through your head, or the production of an intellectual thought. You can also see thinking as observing, that is to say, as a registration of the thoughts in your head, as in mindfulness and meditation. So you go for a conscious walk through your mind. And in addition to thinking being a form of observation, you can employ it as a mode of action: *I'm going to think about something.* That's something you can learn; you can train your thinking ability. And in the end, you can surrender yourself to your own thinking process. That's maybe a bit further down the line, but that is my ideal: that you've developed a mind in which the right thought comes up at the right moment.

Thinking properly creates space in your mind. Once you have that space, you'll be more successful at achieving your goals. I'm not against achieving goals or performing well; I'm against the imbalance that occurs when people are trapped in the drive to achieve. Maybe your goal is to achieve more harmony in your family, or to be happy. It can be anything you choose. As long as you think in a way that allows your mind to be your friend in achieving your goal.

▸ How Do We Befriend Our Minds?

Through practice. Look, if you weren't very good at reading in school, you were never told to just forget about reading. Instead you'd practice. The same applies to thinking. Learning to think begins with asking questions. For example: Why are you doing what you do? What is its purpose? I give my clients exercises that help them think about themes such as gratitude, courage, or regret. They take about half an hour to complete, at least. Which brings me to another success paradox: People often think the exercises sound good, but that they don't have time. The point is to make the time and space. You can also help another person rise above the paradox of success via conversations, which afford you moments to think together. For example, there is a line of thinking in the interview we are having right now, and we are shaping it together through conscious choices. I very much like to practice changing gears: a bit of philosophy, then asking some interesting questions, or just letting some silence in for a bit.

▸ So It's Actually About Achieving Freedom of Mind.

Well, that is indeed my ideal, for as long as you are caught in your thinking, you are not free. If you want too much and want it too badly, wanting becomes a problem and "your will" becomes an adversary. You have focused on something in the future that prevents you from looking further, or around you, in the now. You seize upon your goal and it prevents you from being patient and blocks openness. Sometimes I think that "wanting in a good way" has more to do with being able to receive. I think we have become a little too traditionally masculine in our wanting. We are very results-oriented and want to enforce things—may even demand them. And we identify ourselves with any failure we suffer. If we could succeed in wanting from a willingness to receive, it would lead to more gratitude and appreciation.

ᐅ Can You Give an Example?

There was a situation at work when I was becoming increasingly annoyed by the plethora of emails I was receiving from a client. We had to meet up at one point, and he proposed that we meet in my hometown, and that I be the one to arrange the location. This annoyed me, because I wanted to deal with this as quickly as possible and didn't want to spend time on the logistics. Only when I thought about it in a quiet moment did I realize the other side of it: Here is a client willing to travel to the other side of the country at whatever time suits me, and all I have to do is arrange for a nice location. Looking at it that way, I realized it was actually everything I wanted. But when you're busy and feeling like there's no time to handle

anything, you don't see what's actually already there. To be open to this ability to receive is a different form of wanting.

ᐅ How Can We Open Up Like That?

Good question. It might sound a little vague, but in the end it is about surrendering control and not knowing exactly what's going to happen. This allows you to create space so things can happen to you. It also requires letting go without expecting some form of payback. If you succeed, then suddenly you can look at things differently. And you may just receive something that you've wanted for a long time.

ᐅ That's Not Easy.

No, because that road is full of discomfort. And tolerating discomfort is something we really need to get better at. We naturally move away from anything uncomfortable. But what happens if you let yourself experience the discomfort? It depends on what your purpose is in tolerating it. If you do it with the idea that it will bring you something good, it will not give you anything besides more discomfort. But if you are actually open to the experience, you will gain a richer connection to reality. And you will start noticing lots of things around you that you didn't see before, but actually are all part of—and even the path to—what you desire. Keep asking questions instead of searching for answers. Because if you get good at seeing interesting questions, what's happening is always interesting.

THINKING ABOUT THINKING

》 **Have there been moments recently where you would have liked to have had a bit more time and space to think? When was this?**

_____

_____

_____

》 **What prevented you from taking the time and space to think?**

_____

_____

_____

》 **How could taking the time and space to think benefit you? In what areas of your life?**

_____

_____

_____

》 **What do you have to do or change in your life to be able to have more time and space to think?**

_____

_____

_____

Beauty

IS IN THE

Ordinary

— DIRK DE WACHTER

LET'S PUT IT OFF FOR ONE MORE DAY

BY FLEUR BAXMEIER

"Sometimes problems work themselves out," our parents would tell us when we obsessed over our troubles. And they were right: When you wait a bit, situations change. Here are some benefits to the occasional "wait-and-see."

> **"You must postpone problems; then they mostly go away on their own."**
>
> —Simon Carmiggelt, Dutch author

EMBRACE YOUR DAYDREAMS

Have you ever noticed that the best ideas surface when you're on the bus, doing dishes, or in the shower? According to Paul Loomans, Dutch author of *Time Surfing*, that's thanks to our subconscious. During downtime, our brains have the time to make associations and sift through similar situations.

SIT AND THINK

In today's society, we think highly of people who act quickly, but in Greek and Roman times, wise leaders were encouraged to sit and think the whole day, collecting as much information as possible. Only when it was absolutely necessary did they act.

TRICK YOURSELF

It may sound counterintuitive, but try overloading your to-do list with tasks. The trick is to choose the right projects to place at the top of your list, so you can still be productive while happily avoiding everything else. It's called structured procrastination.

TIME WELL SPENT

Speakers and stand-up comedians have long known that success depends on when and how long you pause. It is not important to do something fast-fast-fast, but to do it well. And sometimes *well* takes just a bit more time.

LET IT SINK IN

Sometimes it feels like you mind can rest only when you've completed every item on your to-do list. But everything doesn't need to be solved immediately: Look at a problem first, then let your feelings sink in and experience them without immediately thinking of solutions. Sometimes while you're caring for yourself, the problem solves itself.

SWITCH YOUR FOCUS

Our first instinct is often to hang in there, show initiative, and up the pressure. But actually in moments such as these, taking a break is a better idea, says Loomans, who is also a Zen master and trainer. He recommends doing something else and revisiting the issue a day later.

REWARD YOURSELF

A Procrastination Research Conference held in 2017 at DePaul University in Chicago revealed that one out of every five people can be categorized as "chronic procrastinators." Start with small steps. "Split up big tasks into smaller tasks—this is how you get an overview," says psychologist Greetje Stomp from the Netherlands. "With less pressure, we experience success sooner and that is another motivator to keep moving forward."

DO AWAY WITH GUILT

Procrastination and guilt are unfortunately a golden combination, yet unnecessarily so. During moments of procrastination, you often finish other tasks: laundry, cleaning the house, paying bills, research for another project, answering emails. Write down all of the tasks that you actually *did* do.

Chapter 2

LOVE YOUR IMPERFECT BODY

ONE OF THE THINGS THAT IS VERY DIFFERENT between the two of us (Irene and Astrid) is the way we think about our bodies. We both worked for many years at fashion magazines—publications that are not known for cultivating the most realistic body images. But there were other factors that shaped our perspectives, even before we stepped into our careers. Irene, for instance, was brought up in a household where her mother was always dieting. Irene saw every fad diet come and go, and having a parent who always talked about her weight had an effect on her. Even now, she still finds herself obsessing over the number on the bathroom scale from time to time. Astrid's approach to her body is much more relaxed. She didn't have the same influences that Irene had growing up. When Astrid thinks about her body in relation to what she eats and how much, it comes from a place of wanting to make healthy choices, rather than with the intention to lose weight or get thinner.

Realizing how our childhoods influence the way we think about our bodies made us aware of the examples we set for our children, and other young people in our lives. We believe that *every body* is amazing, and even if we don't always wake up feeling that way about ourselves, it is the message we strive to embrace, choose to share, and try to model. It's a complicated relationship, but our bodies show up for us, every single day of our lives, and that's worth appreciating.

BE KIND TO YOUR BODY

BY OTJE VAN DER LELIJ

*Being critical of one's body is common,
but loving it again is possible if you can figure out
how to look at it in a different way.*

Many of my childhood memories are physical ones. In one, I'm playing on the riverbed of the Loire in France. Barefoot, I stomp across the shallow river. I build dams with slippery rocks, and the water, warmed by the sun, flows softly through my fingers. I wasn't in my head, but in my body. I *was* my body. But as I grew older, I became more and more in my head. In school I spent hours bent over thick tomes, taking notes. At home, I fed myself with literature, newspapers, and films. French philosopher Descartes's famous theorem *cogito, ergo sum* ("I think, therefore I am") was my forgotten body's proxy. But I also noticed how much importance our society attaches to a beautiful body. So when I did pay attention to my appearance, it was not in a "feeling" way but in a "judging" way: My knees weren't pretty; my stomach wasn't flat enough. Even after I decided it shouldn't matter, I'd sometimes startle at my reflection and wonder if that was really me.

HEAD OVER BODY

Australian philosopher Damon Young agrees that we're becoming alienated from our bodies in today's world. "Society makes a major demand on our minds," he says. "People spend a large part of their working day talking, reading, and typing; there isn't much physical labor. Movement is minimal: pressing screens and buttons, making phone calls. Of course we still have a body, but its contribution to our life is limited." We're becoming more and more in our heads, and less and less in our bodies.

SEEING BUT NOT FEELING

The virtual world is also responsible for this "discorporealization," writes Dutch philosopher Ad Verbrugge. In the virtual biotope where we spend a large part of the day, we're in a space we can't touch, he observes. Our eyes and ears are stimulated, but our other senses (touch, smell) fade into the background. We see images of a beach on Bali passing by online, but we don't breathe in the fresh air or feel the sand under our feet. We scroll through the photo album of someone else's life, but we may fail to notice that this person is actually deeply unhappy— something we'd see much sooner if they were physically present. Through all that scrolling and swiping, Verbrugge says, we're becoming alienated from the corporeal dimension of life.

MIRRORS

"The disconnect that people can feel regarding their bodies also has to do with the attributes that we assign to certain body types," says Canadian psychologist and body image researcher Jessica Alleva of Maastricht University in the Netherlands. "For example, media often associates obesity with laziness and lack of self-control, and society recognizes wrinkles as symbolizing old age. If you have wrinkles and you feel young, or you're a bit overweight and very active, then you don't recognize what you've been conditioned to see in the mirror. You become alienated from your own body."

This third-person perspective is informed by the images present everywhere in society of what a body should look like. But, according to Alleva, that ideal picture is far from realistic. "Scientists admit that the 'ideal image' is more unreal now than ever before," she says. "Women must be slim, fit, and muscular—but not too much so. They must have large breasts and a narrow waist, and always look young and youthful." It's an unattainable ideal that women are confronted with every day. Perfect bodies wave and smile at us from billboards or online ads, implicitly or explicitly selling the message that *this* body is important for success and happiness in love and at work. "It's difficult not to be influenced," Alleva says. "Even though you know that the images are unrealistic, you internalize them. You subconsciously compare your own body with the manipulated idealized image."

I once worked at a fashion magazine, so I know how often the images are Photoshopped. And I think: *Come on, don't be so superficial, surely you're not sensitive to all these images of artificial beauty anymore?* But then I realize it affects me more than I thought. I don't exactly cheer when I'm standing in front of the mirror. Most of my vacation snapshots are safely hidden away in my archives. If I spot a double chin, a roll of fat, or grimace, I delete the photo. That's not who I am, is it? Or rather, who I want to be? But those pictures probably just show me the way I actually look sometimes, the physical "imperfections" that belong to me. So why do I find it so uncomfortable to be confronted with that? Surely real life includes making mistakes and being less attractive, too?

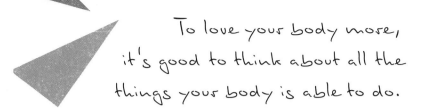

To love your body more, it's good to think about all the things your body is able to do.

LOOKING FROM THE OUTSIDE

"There are quite a few challenges related to the outsider's gaze," Alleva says.

It's disempowering to allow your self-esteem to depend on the judgment of the other, or on society. "Women who look at themselves from the outside (*Am I good enough? Do I look beautiful to other people?*) are more insecure about their bodies," says Alleva. "They are more likely to suffer from eating disorders and are more likely to consider plastic surgery to 'fix' perceived flaws. Even in intimate situations, a woman will experience less pleasure if she's paying too much attention to how she looks, because she is thinking from the point of view of the other person (*Do they find me attractive?*) instead of focusing on herself (*What do I like? What gives me pleasure?*). What's more, she'll have less awareness of her own physical arousal, and will end up also enjoying sex less. The body becomes like a prison, with you trapped inside in the task of achieving an unattainable ideal, and when you don't manage to achieve it—almost always the case—you feel like you're a failure."

SO MUCH BEAUTY

To love your body more, it's good to think about all the things your body is able to do, Alleva learned during her research. In one study, she instructed women with a negative body image to write about what their bodies are capable of and why they are grateful for that. "Women find it difficult to look at their bodies that way," Alleva says. "It's not something we're used to doing." The women spent three periods of fifteen minutes writing. "Each writing assignment had a different focus," Alleva explains. "In one, the women wrote about health: The body can digest food, absorb vitamins, and heal from injuries. Another focused on creativity: You can dance, paint, and write with your body. They also wrote about their senses, physical achievements, and what the body can do in relating to others: You can hug and cuddle, make love, and make eye contact. After the three exercises, the women already had a more positive body image and felt better about how they looked—an effect that was retained a month later."

My own relationship to my body changed after becoming a mother. Though I recognize that the child-bearing process can have the opposite effect for some, I became kinder to my body. For me it was about a mental shift—from thinking about how my body looks to how it functions. I found it nothing short of a miracle that my two girls grew in my body, were fed by my body, and still are wrapped in hugs by my body every day. What I was not yet as conscious of is that I also use my body to dance, write, and make music. And that it's actually quite special that my body is so capable of indicating to me when I'm overdoing it or feeling inspired.

My body is much more than the aesthetic object that I've always been critical of for not living up to the beauty ideal. It plays a major role in everything that makes my life worthwhile. My body is actually my best friend.

READING FACES

"Many people think that once you're satisfied with your body, you'll 'give up,' as it were," Alleva says. "But it works the other way around: The more you love your body, the better you'll want to take care of it."

I can relate to that, too. I've started eating healthier, exercising more, and putting the brakes on quicker when things are stressing me out. And I'll definitely pass on interventions like Botox, which is becoming too easily compared to getting a haircut. Never mind that deliberate beauty always has something stiff and determined about it, research has shown that facial muscles play an important role in communicating: They are important for reading as well as feeling emotions. We recognize emotions by imitating them very subtly. Botox disrupts that imitation process by paralyzing your facial muscles, thereby disguising your own emotions *and* limiting your ability to see others. Switching off one of my body's functions isn't being kind to it.

AT HOME IN YOUR BODY

My relationship with my body has improved even more since I started exercising and meditating. When I'm on my racing bike or meditating, I *am* my body again and I do not judge it. It seems as if the distance I always felt from my body has become smaller. We are so wrapped up in our heads that it's really important to feel our bodies now and then.

According to Young, who practices yoga, you gain a more complete picture of your own body on the yoga mat. "By slowly stretching and bending you regain a sense of your body because you become aware of what usually is unconscious," he says. "Not only visually, but also from the inside out." You experience a richer idea of yourself, which Young compares to a "kind of interior design": You start to feel at home again in your interior.

I recognize myself in these words. When I stretch or meditate, I become aware of muscle groups I had forgotten I had. I feel the air flow in and out of my lungs, and notice where tension is residing in my body. In such moments I feel very physical, very close to myself. Just like on that beautiful day on the riverbed of the Loire where I played so happily as a kid. I had no body then; I *was* my body.

When I'm on my racing bike or meditating, I am my body again and I do not judge it.

My body plays a major role in everything that makes my life worthwhile.

LEARN MORE ABOUT BODY IMAGE

▸ *Embrace* Many women express dissatisfaction with their bodies because their shape doesn't match some unattainable ideal. "Lose weight, eliminate wrinkles, fight cellulite. We're constantly forced to become someone else," says Taryn Brumfitt, the Australian founder of the Body Image Movement. With her documentary, *Embrace*, she hopes to contribute to a more positive body image in women.

▸ "Suddenly, my body" American poet, feminist, and activist Eve Ensler has always lived in her head. In a poetic speech for TEDWomen (available on YouTube), she talks about the distance she always felt from her body, and how her work in the Congo and her illness helped her to get in touch again with the embodiment of being human.

NEED A NEW PERSPECTIVE? VISIT A MUSEUM

German philosopher Rebekka Reinhard writes that we particularly like what we are conditioned to like, or what is familiar to us. And the fewer things we are exposed to, the harder it is to judge what's beautiful and what's not. Reinhard writes that beauty is very much like food: Only someone with lots of culinary experience can judge whether a poached goose liver terrine with pears, kohlrabi, and smoked pigeon breast goes better with a beer or a Riesling wine. According to her, you can develop your skills of discernment with regard to your own body by going to museums (or looking at art books at the library!) more often. Borrow the eyes of an artist—Rubens, for example. For him, large bodies signaled opulence, an open mind, a carefree spirit, and joyfulness. If you can see that, Reinhard argues, you may also look at your own body in a friendlier manner.

Rest the Stress Away

BY ANNEKE BOTS

It can hit you like a ton of bricks. Everything suddenly becomes too much and you find yourself heading for a burnout. Anneke Bots follows architect Lisa in her search for a solution and discovers some surprising insights.

On September 5 at 11 a.m., the lights went out for 27-year-old architect Lisa. It was her first day back at the office after a vacation in Bali. She had begun working at a small firm eighteen months earlier. It was her first job and she had thrown herself into her work with enthusiasm, never saying no to anything, and feeling like she should be able to do it all.

Her plan had been to relax and recharge on the tropical island. But she hadn't succeeded. Quite the contrary. "I was having panic attacks," she says. "My memory was like a sieve, and I wasn't in the mood for *anything*." She longed to be home, but when her family welcomed her at the airport, she wasn't even happy to see them. "I was empty. I couldn't feel anything anymore."

Two days later, on that fateful September 5, she went back to work. She turned on her computer and "my fingers started tingling," she recalls. "I felt lightheaded and had trouble breathing. I wanted to go outside, but I could barely manage that. After a lot of effort, I finally made it outside, and all I could do was cry. After that I didn't go back to work for six months. It was the deepest hole I had ever been in."

EMPTY

Lisa was completely exhausted. In the first week, she couldn't even take a shower standing up. In the first month, she couldn't face going out for groceries, so others did it for her. "When you're in the midst of a burnout, your body is completely depleted and your brain is in a state of chaos," she says.

Carolien Hamming, director at the Chronic Stress Reversal Center, founded by psychotherapist and psychologist Sonja van Zweden in the Netherlands, explains: "When you work constantly and do not relax enough, you end up exhausting your body's resources and deregulating your hormonal system. Once you become aware of this, it becomes clear that you need to change your behavior. Psychological treatment alone is not enough." She doesn't agree with the advice usually given to someone with a burnout, which is to start working on their problems immediately, or to visit a therapist to hash out their childhood. Such advice is based on the premise that the stress is caused by the mind. "Which is understandable, because there are often psychological issues too, but first of all your body has to recover and your brain has to be functioning a bit better," she explains. "Once your body regains its balance, the depressed feelings and panic attacks usually also subside."

Psychologist and mindfulness teacher Karin Rekvelt has also noticed that many therapists focus too much on the mind. As a result, patients often learn a lot of valuable things, such as the

Learn to simply do nothing without feeling embarrassed.

fact that it's good to try to be less of a perfectionist, to say no more often, or to set realistic goals for themselves, but they're still stuck in a negative spiral despite the therapy. "It's essential to also gain insight into what stress does to your body and what happens when your body has become deregulated by long-term overextension," Rekvelt says. "The physical component is so important, because you can be aware of the stress factors in your life, like the pressures of work for example, but it's crucial to understand that it's the incorrect response to these stress factors that are draining your body."

Lisa visited Rekvelt, but not before seeing a psychologist that her GP had referred her to. "Right from the get-go, the psychologist started digging around for the psychological causes of my problems," she says. "I couldn't handle that kind of conversations at all. I wasn't able to see anything in perspective." Lisa didn't go back after that first session and eventually found her way to Rekvelt instead. She had experienced her burnout in an emphatically physical way, Lisa says. "So for me, the explanation that my body was overextended and therefore lost its balance made a lot of sense. I couldn't actually relate to my negative thoughts at all; I had never felt depressed before. Now I know I had simply made it impossible to rest, I was 'on' all the time. Actually resting became more and more unnatural; it had become a trigger for feeling restless. As I started recovering, my somber thoughts vanished. Learning to do nothing was the most important thing for me."

STRESS MECHANISM

There's nothing wrong with working hard; it's the working hard without giving your body rest that's the problem. "It's all about striking a healthy balance between expending energy and recharging again," Hamming says. "The stress mechanism is an activation system that ensures we have enough energy to get out of bed and be alert and active. The stress hormones adrenaline and cortisol play a big part in this. If you are under stress or when you're playing a sport, you need more energy and the stress mechanism steps up its efforts. When you are resting, your body recovers, especially when you're sleeping: You need that time to recharge so you wake up ready for the next day. If you don't allow this to happen, you're overextending your body's resources."

It's not like it happens all at once, of course, but there are plenty of signs on the road there: tiredness, headaches, somber feelings, anxiety attacks, worrying, sleepless nights, not being in the mood to do anything (even fun things) and physical ailments that won't go away. These are all warning signals of a system about to hit a burnout. Most people will then stop working. If you keep working, you tire your body out even more, until it reaches a point where it simply says, *Stop, I can't take it anymore.* You could be overcome by a panic attack in the middle of the street, freezing you on the spot. The tiniest setback could make you fall apart. An appointment being canceled, a sneer from a coworker, something trivial, can make you burst out crying and

not be able to stop. "You can keep going for a very long time on willpower and last reserves," says Hamming, "but the moment comes when your body gives up. It's like a telephone that keeps managing to charge its battery only a little bit at a time, and some functionalities don't work properly anymore. You have barely any energy left, and slowly gaps appear in your mind. You can't think clearly anymore and can't remember things. All kinds of substances in your brain are out of whack, which makes you unstable and emotional, and you probably even have trouble recognizing yourself at times. Once you've reached this point, it won't matter if you remove the stress factors. Your body won't be able to recover with a good weekend of rest or a few weeks of vacation." Once you've crossed this line, recovery takes a long time: Count on six to nine months to come back from a nervous breakdown and between six months and two years for a burnout.

WHERE'S THE "OFF" BUTTON?

The key to healing from a stress overload is first of all learning how to rest. After that, you can work on self-management, which will prevent you from reaching this state again. Resting isn't easy if you feel super stressed at the smallest provocation and can't find the off button. "It's quite a challenge to find out what helps you personally the most, but it's generally a good starting point to accept that it's okay that you're not okay and not to feel guilty about that," Hamming says. "Rest up, and learn to simply do nothing without feeling embarrassed, but keep some structure in your day. Loaf about, but try not to worry a lot. Being out in fresh air, taking a walk, visiting a friend—those things usually do a world of good. But for

people with a burnout, too much physical activity is actually not a good idea. When you're moving around, your body creates extra stress hormones and that's exactly what you don't need. To recover, the repair system in your body needs to be dominant. Seek out social support; talking to friends can be really good. But also remember, when you're in the midst of a burnout even *that* can generate stress, so listen carefully to your body and see what works for you."

"Take your body seriously when it tells you it's tired, and take a nap," adds doctor and burnout coach Gijs Schraa. "Don't dismiss the urge. It's a good thing to let your body get used

to sleeping again. Rest is important to build up stores of energy." Schraa recommends you take a bit of distance in order to keep stress down to a healthy low level. "Make sure you think about what you're doing and how you're doing it on a regular basis and before things derail. Most importantly, plan moments of rest."

WIND IN YOUR HAIR

But being this relaxed—resting and taking naps—is easier said than done when you're used to going that extra mile. For Lisa, it took a long time before she could activate the relaxation mode. "I knew I was supposed to take it easy, but I was still caught up in an activity vortex," she says. "I couldn't stop thinking and my body was stuck in overdrive, which created a lot of anxiety and kept me from sleeping full nights. It was a vicious cycle, and I wasn't managing to break out of it on my own. I thought of myself as a pretty insightful person but now I was clearly in need of help. I needed someone to tell me, 'It's okay, let it go, let go of it all.' Rekvelt was a tremendous help: She used an anatomy book to show me what was wrong with my body. That was perfect for me—I always like to know how things work in practical terms. Starting from the 'off mode,' in which I wasn't able to do any little thing, I slowly rebuilt my life. Very slowly. It took five months before I was able to relax again and sometimes sleep an entire night. I watched TV series endlessly, read books, and tried to write about my experience. Every day I took a walk; I started with ten-minute walks, in the end I was walking three miles (5 km) every day."

Rekvelt also advises you to always listen to your body, whether you're recovering from a burnout or feel like you're at risk. "Listen carefully to it and take it seriously, no matter what the people around you tell you," she says. "This is essential. Take the time to observe the world with your senses: let the wind blow through your hair, feel the sun on your skin, walk in the sand with bare feet. Be conscious of all your senses: What do I smell? What do I taste? Get back in touch with your body."

Lisa's recovery process continued with ups and downs. For a while she was scared she was never going to be her old self again, but she has since regained confidence in her body. She feels energized again and is back at her job, with a healthier outlook. "I've learned to listen to my body," she says. "I take a timeout when my body tells me I need it."

TIPS FROM THE COACH

What can you do when you're overstressed or hovering on the edge of a nervous breakdown? Here are some tips from Karin Rekvelt:

- ● Accept that stress is a natural part of life. When you feel tired, edgy, and depleted, give that feeling some space.

- ● Only do what you have to. Cut all non-essential activities from your agenda, in work as well as in your private life. Cancel social appointments, too—even those that seem like a lot of fun. They cost more energy than you realize.

- ● Make sure you sleep well. Slowing down in the evening helps you fall asleep: Listen to calm music, read a book, and teach yourself to do relaxing exercises before you go to bed.

- ● Consider doing a mindfulness or yoga class.

- ● Don't think of stress as your enemy, but as a fascinating process that engages you to listen to your mind and body.

Floral Fun

This DIY paper flower by Dutch
illustrator Valesca van Waveren requires
very little assembly—and no water!
Just punch out the individual pieces
from the page and fit them together
to make a three-dimensional
paper bloom. Give it as a gift
to yourself, just because.

ILLUSTRATION
VALESCA VAN WAVEREN

MY LOVE

I

My love is not like the rose,
Nor the languid lady-lily,
Nor the pansy, pensive-faced,
Nor the drooping "daffy-dilly."

II

She's not like the pale snowdrop,
Fears of frailty in us waking,
Nor the shrinking violet,
For the shade the sun forsaking.

III

I can only liken her
To the brave and bonnie heather—
Hardy, wholesome, and not made
For a hothouse or fine weather.

—Marie Hedderwick Browne, 1893

NATURE ACCEPTS YOU AS YOU ARE.

— GARY FERGUSON

BY SJOUKJE VAN DE KOLK

Nature is the only thing in his life that never really disappoints, says Gary Ferguson, author of The Eight Master Lessons of Nature. *The beauty of it is that everyone can rediscover that feeling that we had as children, when we were enchanted by bugs and pretty leaves.*

❱ Why Do You Love Nature So Much?

I grew up in a fairly industrialized city and I still remember the sense of wonder that I had as a child when I got to be out in nature—what it felt like to climb a tree and play in the backyard or a nearby park. I had a difficult family situation, and nature became the place where I felt at home and where I felt safe. By the time I was grown, I realized that nature, unlike other things in life, was always the same as, or even better than, the last time I had experienced it. That sense of comfort was always there. It's the only thing in my life that never really disappoints me, especially when times are rough.

❱ Was That Feeling of Coming Home to Nature Conscious?

Many of us have an inborn tendency to enjoy being in nature. Small children are amazed by little beetles and other small animals that we grown-ups have long stopped noticing. A child experiences nature—even a small backyard or a window box—as a source of beauty and mystery. Unfortunately, that feeling disappears as you get older. We live in a culture that appreciates predictability and control, and the acquisition of material things. We start doubting the feelings we had as a child and we drift further away from them.

❱ Can We Get That Feeling Back?

Yes, we all have the capacity to rediscover it. For many years, I worked with a therapy program for young people. The program took them to the mountain wilderness for two months. In the beginning they were often scared—of the place itself, of the animals, the sounds, of the lack of comfort. But again and again we saw change within two weeks. Nature did the same with them as it did with me when I was a child. They felt safe and accepted. Their only job was to use the setting to help understand the world and to experience who they were. That is what nature can do.

❱ What Is the Most Important Lesson We Can Learn from Nature?

That everything is connected. We walk under the trees that give us the oxygen we need. There are millions of bacteria in your stomach that help you to digest food. Sunlight triggers the production of serotonin, which helps you focus during the day, and also creates vitamin D in your body, which you need for strong bones. In the United States, there's this societal obsession with the rugged individual; the one that doesn't need anybody. But it's an illusion. If we build a society where everyone lives for themselves and grabs what they can, it will lead to chaos in

We are a unique and smart species that can do a lot, but we literally owe our lives to what we are surrounded by.

the end. If we can learn to see that connection, though—if we were to wake up every morning thinking about how we are all connected, just imagine the good we could do.

» How Do You Practice That?
One basic exercise you can try is every time you see a plant or tree, realize that the oxygen you breathe comes from it. *That* tree is essential for the actual fact that you can breathe. We are a unique and smart species that can do a lot, but we literally owe our lives to what we are surrounded by. You don't need an extravagant ritual: simply pause for a moment to realize that it works that way.

» You Also Write That Nature Helps You Look Outside Yourself.
That is true. Our social and economic systems are all about improving and optimizing ourselves, making it constantly on our minds. Nature can pull you out of that feeling. A sunset, a flock of birds, a flowering garden—they stop you from feeling that you are the center of the universe, and help to remove the responsibility that the feeling carries with it. At the sight of a flock of birds, you don't need to do anything except observe. It doesn't sound good for the ego to be pushed aside like that, but actually it's such a relief. You don't have to be the center of everything and you are not responsible for everything. It's very healing.

» How Does the Healing Work?
I experienced this very strongly after my first wife, Jane, passed away. She died in an accident during a canoe trip. The wilderness was a place I loved, but at that time it became in my mind the cause of my wife's death. That was very confusing. I was feeling very sorry for myself, and it felt like the world was an unfair place—which is all part of mourning. When I accepted that, I began seeing the beauty of nature again. I was living in a beautiful place in the forest and the birds that were there when Jane was alive were still there. The same trees were growing. At first you wonder how it can be possible, how the world can continue. But it just happens. If you spend a lot of time in nature, you can't help but begin to understand the cycle of life and death. It doesn't necessarily make it easier, but the realization does give you a chance to be more aware of the preciousness of every day.

» What Is the Biggest Takeaway?
Go outside more often! Several studies show what a walk in nature does for you: Your attention shifts from yourself to everything that's happening around you. When you realize that you are not the center of the world, but that you are on the edge of it, it brings peace. And you don't necessarily have to know why that is.

I'm slowing
down the tune

I never liked it fast

You want to
get there soon

I want to get
there last

—Leonard Cohen

The Wonders of Walking

BY BERNICE NIKIJULUW

As far back as antiquity, the ancient Greeks knew the benefits of walking in nature. Today, taking a stroll outside is indeed still good for body and mind.

was sitting in the car next to my new love, an Englishman with whom I had gone to Yorkshire, United Kingdom, for the weekend. I wondered about whether we could stop to explore the beautiful landscape on foot. We'd left London early that morning and had been driving for at least an hour through lush green hills, dotted with dry stone walls and lots of sheep. My Englishman responded with amazement. It had not occurred to him at all.

ACROSS THE ENGLISH LANDSCAPE

The Englishman and I have now been together for more than a quarter of a century. That day in Yorkshire, I'd convinced him that just looking at a landscape through a car window is not nearly as much fun as being out in it. Together, we have now crossed large parts of England and Wales on foot, as well as regions even farther away from home. When we lived in London, we both had full-time office jobs and we used the weekends to get out into nature. We'd book a bed-and-breakfast in a small village and buy a detailed map showing all the footpaths in the area. Called "public rights of way," these paths often run across farmyards and private estates. We planned a route (hopefully with a pub at the halfway point), laced up our hiking boots, and set off. At the end of the weekend, with tired legs, healthy lungs, and an overall feeling of calm, we would return to London with renewed energy.

WALKING TO CLEAR YOUR MIND

We now live in Amsterdam, and though daily life is far more easy-going, we miss the complete relaxation of a walking weekend. It is harder to find untouched nature here, so we wander out less. But I've discovered it is possible to go for beautiful walks wherever you are, even if, like me, you live in a heavily populated area. Thankfully, I have a flexible work schedule, so if I anticipate a few good-weather days, I can plan my schedule to spend a weekday morning walking in the dunes. And during a recent Christmas holiday, I dragged my family out to the rural southeast of the Netherlands to walk the Pieterpad, an ancient pilgrims'

"I started walking the Camino because I felt the need to break out," she says. "Although I did the walk alone, I never felt lonely. On this route you meet lots of special people with interesting stories. You also meet people who just do a portion of the route while on vacation, as a completely different experience. I find that it takes a couple of weeks to really get into the flow: The struggle is over and you find a kind of inner peace. Since coming home, I still try to walk every day. If I don't for a couple of days, I feel it in my legs: They get stiff from sitting still. Walking awakens and heals my body and soul."

HINDE JOLDERSMA *has walked the pilgrim route to Santiago de Compostela from the South of France. She also manages hindewalk.nl, a website with overnight addresses for walkers.*

For Wordsworth, walking sparked off the creative process that inspired his poems.

footpath that runs the length of the country, for two whole days. It was a spur of the moment thing: I saw that we had a few bright frosty days coming up, so I booked rooms in a farmhouse bed-and-breakfast halfway through a stretch of the Pieterpad, which meant we could cover a distance of about 15.5 miles (25 km) in two manageable parts. After an hour and a half in the train, we walked through a frozen fairy-tale landscape where the sun's long rays made the view at every step even nicer to look at. In the evening in the cozy kitchen of the bed-and-breakfast, we ate a meal that had been prepared for us by our hostess and then went out in the icy cold to admire the incredibly starry sky. What enhanced the joy of that particular walk was the fact that we also had a destination; we were expected somewhere at a certain time and felt accomplished by the end of the journey.

While pilgrimages were historically religious in nature, the modern pilgrimage is undertaken for a variety of reasons: finding meaning, self-reflection, regaining physical strength after an illness or burnout, to support someone else, or just because the adventure beckons.

SOURCE OF INSPIRATION

The British walking tradition may have begun with William Wordsworth, the wandering poet from the beautiful Lake District. During his era, walking was not considered necessary for someone of his class, but Wordsworth understood that it as a way to feel at one with nature. For him, walking sparked off the creative process that inspired his poems.

Swiss-born philosopher Jean-Jacques Rousseau discovered the joys of walking before Wordsworth. He claimed that he could only think, give form to something, or otherwise create properly when he walked alone. In the open nature, inspiration came naturally, while the sight of his writing desk made him feel overcome by aversion and boredom.

One of the most enthusiastic walkers ever was American philosopher and writer Henry David Thoreau, who walked through the woods for four hours at least every day. Thoreau worried about the wilderness disappearing and humanity losing contact with nature. His essay "Walking" is a plea for walking in untouched nature, because he felt that it was the only way to feel free in a society where sitting down had become more common than moving.

FOREST BATH

Wordsworth, Rousseau, and Thoreau were on to something. Walking in nature is good for the body and soul. Together with his research team, Professor Yoshifumi Miyazaki of the Center for Environment, Health, and Field Sciences at Chiba University in Japan conducted an extensive study into the effect of walking in forests compared with walking through busy city centers. You guessed it: The woodland walkers felt more relaxed than the city walkers. Also, their levels of the stress hormone cortisol decreased significantly along with their blood pressure and heart rate. Introduced in 1982 as a slogan to promote the health of city dwellers, the term *shinrin-yoku* (literally: "absorbing the forest's atmosphere") was coined by Japan's Forestry Agency. According to Japanese scientists, not only is fresh air beneficial to our health, the oils that trees and plants release—the phytoncides—are, too. *Shinrin-yoku* improves our moods, reduces stress, increases resistance to illness, and reduces the risk of cardiovascular disease. This meditative way of walking in nature is now popular in the United States, where specially trained forest therapy guides teach walkers how to use all their senses: feeling the wind, touching the trees, smelling all the scents, and noticing the vibrancy of the colors.

The whole world seems to have rediscovered the many benefits of walking. Everywhere, there is evidence that it can make you healthier and happier. And the good thing is, anyone with a pair of healthy legs can do it, and it won't cost a thing. Although, of course, you could always hire a professional to help you learn how to relax and reflect if you want; the number of walking coaches is growing steadily and you can learn to walk mindfully or take part in guided walking meditation.

The business community sees the benefits, too: A refreshed employee is a productive employee, so smart bosses encourage lunchtime walks and some even organize walking meetings. Dutch psychologist and professor Agnes van den Berg encourages GPs and physiotherapists to go on "green walks" with their patients. And in psychiatry, walking therapy is regarded as a beneficial treatment, especially for people with symptoms of depression. Walking is a way to slow life down, to think things over, to take in the environment, to give your creativity a boost, to relax spiritually, and to stay in physical shape.

> It was my ex who always wanted to walk," she says. "It didn't matter that much to me. I only started walking after my divorce, initially for the distraction. My head was one big storm, full of disruptive thoughts, but because of the cadence of walking, the rhythm I felt in my body, I managed to find myself again. In the beginning, I walked for hours on the beach, barefoot. But now I walk a lot through the city, straight out my front door. What I used to do on my bike, I now do on foot. It takes more time, but I find that I am more effective during my working hours because I am fresher and can focus better. Slowing down is good for me."
>
> *Journalist and massage therapist*
> **BIANCA BARTELS** *"learned to walk"*
> *when her relationship ended.*

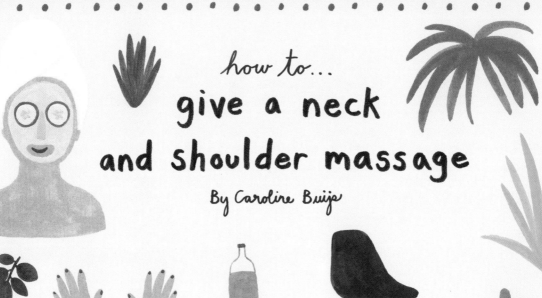

how to...
give a neck
and shoulder massage

By Caroline Buijs

What you need: A chair, warm hands, short fingernails (take off any rings, if necessary), massage oil if desired.

General tip: Massage only the back of the neck and exert pressure only on muscles, never on bones.

1. Invite the person you are going to massage to sit back-to-front on a chair, facing backward and with their arms folded over the backrest.

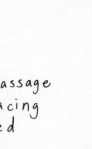

2. Warm up the neck muscles with your ring, middle, and index fingertips. Apply light but firm pressure, moving in small circles along the sides of the neck, from the hairline down the shoulders and back up again.

3. Place your palms on the shoulders on either side of the neck. Use your thumbs to gently push up the skin of the neck. Repeat.

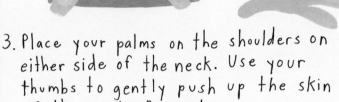

4. If you sense a tension knot, place your thumbs on the knot and your other fingers on the front of the shoulders. Make circular kneading movements, exerting firm but gentle pressure to loosen the tension in the muscles.

5. Move your fingertips in a circular kneading movement over the shoulder blades. When you get to the spine, alternate with the heel of your palm; that's how to exert broader pressure, which feels better.

6. Sometimes a five-minute massage can be enough, but you can always go on for longer.

illustrations Kate Pugsley

DRINKING TEA, A DAILY RITUAL

BY HEDWIG WIEBES

What would you hold on to while selling off your belongings in order to travel the world in a camper van? For one woman, it was her teapot. The daily ritual of drinking tea gave her sense of security that made her feel at home no matter where and how far she traveled.

I drink tea every day. At least twice, and almost always a whole pot. I start the day with green tea in the morning and drink herbal tea the rest of the day. When I travel, I invariably pack a few tea bags (for when there may be a kettle in a hotel room, but otherwise nothing more than a couple of stale bags of black tea and instant coffee)—a cup of my "own" tea feels like a true luxury.

My appreciation for tea began during the two years that I lived my life traveling in a camper van. It was meant to be a simple life, away from the hustle and bustle of the city and, above all, away from all the obligations that came with day-to-day life. But the simple life I had envisioned turned out to be unexpectedly complicated. Maybe that's why people live in houses—because it's actually quite convenient! Things that had been simple, like grocery shopping or going to bed, now took up a lot of time and energy—we shopped in a different store almost every day, attempted to decipher new product packaging, planned where we were going to sleep next (and tried to determine whether we and our vehicle were even allowed there). We scouted the edges of a farming town seeking Wi-Fi like the spoiled yuppies that we were; it seemed like we were constantly packing and unpacking, making use of every cubic centimeter of the van.

Our simple life was not necessarily a quiet or easy life (or maybe we just hadn't adapted yet). But in that same life, in which everything seemed challenging and uncertain, one safe beacon became clear: Even when everything seemed to be going wrong, I had my tea. I would take a sip, sigh deeply, and everything would come back into perspective.

ALWAYS AT HOME

We had said goodbye to almost all of our physical possessions, but my beautiful Chinese cast-iron teapot was definitely going on the road with us. And it turned out that the tea was

When it was cold, I put the teapot on my lap, like a pleasantly heavy hot-water bottle.

not the only thing that sustained me. When it was cold, I put the pot on my lap, like a pleasantly heavy hot-water bottle.

We kept my tea on the top shelf of the only cupboard in the van. I had reached the conclusion that I could do with less in most areas of my life, but this did not include my many boxes and bags of tea. When we hit the road, I took my entire stash with me—a small fortune of brightly colored packages covered in prints, sayings, and promises. It's a bit over the top, but I also recognized that I'm not an indiscriminate hoarder; I actually would drink each of these teas.

I cut open the prettiest boxes into collecting trays and fit three or four bags of each type inside. I sorted by color, as I had discovered that this signifier almost always corresponds to the type of tea, and was left with an exuberant rainbow of tea bags displayed on the shelf of the small cupboard. I kept the rest of my stock in a bag in the roof box on top of the van, and replenished my cupboard stock as needed. "A cup of tea would restore my normality," Douglas Adams writes in *The Hitchhiker's Guide to the Galaxy*. That's how I felt on the road.

Wherever we ended up, whether it was a desolate parking lot or a beach with the most idyllic view, the whistle of the tea kettle reliably brought me home. We closed the curtains, lit a candle, and in moments like that, I felt ridiculously content.

C. S. Lewis, author of The Chronicles of Narnia series, once said that a cup of tea can never be too big (and a book can never be long enough). In Lewis Caroll's *Alice's Adventures in Wonderland* it's "always tea-time." Is that the role of the recurring tea drinking in those fantasy worlds: a way to keep one's feet on the ground? "I say let the world go to hell, but I should always have my tea," wrote Russian novelist Fyodor Dostoevsky. The whole world may be mad, but tea will be our salvation.

HEALTH AND HARMONY

When my partner and I first met, he didn't drink tea. "It's for sick people," he said. Now he wouldn't want to go without. For both of us, it warms body and soul (not to mention, it's delicious). More importantly for me, it's an indicator of whether I am taking good care of myself. If I find myself too busy to go to that small trouble of brewing a pot of tea—preferring instead a drink of plain water—it's a signal to me that something's out of balance, and that I may be overdoing something.

Plus tea has many health benefits. When I first looked at my relationship with tea (when I was packing it all up and arranging the bags by color), I wondered if I was simply drawn to the fancy packaging. But I eventually recognized that the contents were just as important to me. I discovered why I had a preference for certain ingredients at certain times of day. With my limited background in herbalism, I also started collecting my own loose dried herbs and fresh herbs, and began coming up with my own combinations. It's now second nature to me to go for fennel seeds when I suffer from bloating or juniper berries during days with severe PMS. And I know that the bergamot oil in Earl Grey

has an uplifting effect on days when I need a bit of cheer.

It is no surprise that I associate drinking tea with personal warmth. When I was a child, it was already one of my favorite moments of the day: sitting after school at the big table with my mother and sisters around a large, steaming pot of tea. Next to it, a tin of cookies. I didn't realize the value of these moments at the time. They were otherwise ordinary—pleasantly simple, filled with happiness.

Later, every time I made tea for people we met along our travels, I recalled the memory of the big table and family. Except our landscape

was vastly different: My cast-iron pot stood in a hollow of sand or on a tripod of rocks, with everyone sitting cross-legged around it.

Perhaps the secret behind tea lies in the fact that making tea is such a humble act. It can be the center of extravagant ceremonies, like those practiced in many Asian cultures: Reverently bowing figures in elegant dress, who carefully pour the hot liquid into beautifully decorated bowls from which careful sips are taken. In the midst of the chaos of everyday life, it is such a refined, simple act that it is almost spiritual, writes Yasuhiko Murai in the book *Tea in Japan*. British tea traditions also hold a sort of formal reverence. I have never taken part in an organized tea ceremony—they're not really my style.

But maybe my own rituals fill that space in my life: Hand me a huge mug that I can wrap my hands around, and some dark chocolate to go with it.

WHO I AM

Today I am leading a more structured life once again. I didn't go back to living in a city and I've kept obligations down to less than they were before, but a lot is still happening. Too much, on some days. When I feel an imbalance coming on—when I start falling back into old patterns that are too much about achievement and too little about who I am—I turn again to that then simmering kettle, and that warm cup I can cradle in my hands. It's a simple daily ritual that reminds me to take time for the things that are important to me.

Hand me a huge mug that I can wrap my hands around, and some dark chocolate.

Reflect the season's mood; find fresh perspectives.

Chapter 3

LOVE BEING ALONE

BEING ALONE FROM TIME TO TIME TO focus on our own thoughts, hobbies, or favorite food without having to compromise or share is such a treat. But *feeling* alone can be hard, no matter your situation. A wave of loneliness can hit you even in the middle of a crowd, during dinner with a friend, or with a partner sleeping next to you. *Being* alone can be beautiful but *feeling* alone . . . never.

As a divorced parent with shared custody, Irene spends more time on her own than Astrid, who is married with children, and occasionally we have lively discussions about the pros and cons of aloneness. When Irene shares that it can feel a bit sad to arrive home to an empty house after a long day of work with no one there to pour you a cup of tea and ask about your day and to ask about theirs in return, Astrid points out that a full house is not always what you want either. Sometimes she just needs some peace and quiet at the end of a busy day or, better still, an evening or weekend by herself with no one else around. There are obviously cases to be made for both sets of circumstances, and discussing the pros and cons together helps us to realize that. And being alone—or, rather, learning to be together with yourself—is an important life skill.

If you can get to know yourself, and genuinely appreciate your own company, you'll not only be more present and engaged around other people, but you're less likely to feel lonely when a quiet moment settles in.

"Be able to be alone. Lose not the advantage of solitude."

—Thomas Browne (1605-1682)

WE ARE LONELY MORE OFTEN

BY CAROLINE BUIJS

Everyone feels alone sometimes, but when does that feeling turn into loneliness? If you can find that balance, spending time alone also has its advantages.

I hadn't been in a relationship with my boyfriend for very long yet when he went to Latin America for two months, in the summer of 1991. My girlfriends were away on vacation and I was supposed to work through the summer as a flight attendant, but because of a minor infection, it turns out I wasn't allowed to fly. I found myself alone in my apartment in a hot city. There were no cell phones yet, airmail letters took ages, and long-distance phone calls to faraway friends were expensive. It was the first time I remember feeling really lonely. I only left my house for groceries because I couldn't bear the sight of a sun-kissed city in which everyone but me seemed to be having a good time. But after a couple of weeks of self-pity, I decided to find ways to have fun on my own. I joined the library and read the entire oeuvre of Dutch author W. F. Hermans that summer. I discovered the museums. I cycled to the park with my picnic blanket and saw that there were lots of people reading alone, which gave me a comforting sense of connection. In retrospect, it was an educational summer: I learned that I could be friends with myself and have a good time while being on my own. My unbearable loneliness turned into solitude: a positive sort of withdrawal, in which I actually enjoyed being alone.

COLD AS ICE AND CLEAR AS GLASS

What does it feel like to be lonely? Some liken it to being hungry—"like being hungry when everyone around you is readying for a feast," writes English author Olivia Laing in her book *The Lonely City*. "It feels shameful and alarming, and over time these feelings radiate outward, making the lonely person increasingly isolated, increasingly estranged. It hurts, in the way that feelings do. . . . It advances, is what I'm trying to say, cold as ice and clear as glass, enclosing and engulfing." When you feel lonely, it's often because you did not choose to be that way.

"[Being lonely] is a subjective experience that everyone participates in differently, but

It is up to all of us
to build and maintain
a convoy of people.

the crux of the matter is always that you are seeing less of other people than you would like or that the quality of the contact is less than you would like," writes Jenny Gierveld, professor emeritus of sociology at VU Amsterdam via email. "Having fewer contacts than you wish, in terms of everyday social contacts, is called social loneliness," she writes in a blog entry for a foundation that fights against loneliness in communities. "Not having a confidante in your circle of contacts—someone you, for example, can tell things to that shouldn't be told to anyone else—is called emotional loneliness."

A BIT OF THIS, A BIT OF THAT

Often it is not just one thing that makes you feel lonely, but a combination of factors.

Sometimes we're lonely by circumstance. Only children sometimes report feeling lonely (while others feel the complete opposite, since they may be more attuned to actively seeking out close friendships outside of their families). Or, it "could be a personal quality that makes you sensitive to loneliness," says Theo van Tilburg, professor of sociology at VU Amsterdam. "Maybe you're shy or lack self-confidence. Sometimes you lose social connections because you're going through a divorce, or because someone close to you has passed away. Having health problems or being unemployed can play a role, too. But it's also possible for people to have expectations of social contacts which are just too high."

In his book, *A Philosophy of Loneliness*, Norwegian philosopher Lars Svendsen calls this "social perfectionism." People who feel lonely are often both critical of others and of themselves, he writes. As a result, their need for connection with others is not always fulfilled. And, because they are critical of themselves, they don't like being alone either. Trust plays a major role in loneliness, too. Svendsen

HOW TO REACH OUT TO OTHERS

"When you suspect that someone is lonely, go and talk to that person," says sociologist Jenny Gierveld. "Invite them for a cup of coffee or tea. And then listen to their stories. Listen and don't give advice. At some point, the other person will certainly spontaneously start talking about their concerns or fears. Maybe it's loneliness, or maybe something completely different. Keep listening. Never ask directly about possible loneliness in the other person. The word on its own scares people off. What else helps? A regular conversation, a visit. Talking about small things is usually a good start. It's nice if the other person knows you're coming back and that you're always available to listen."

asserts: "The more you trust others, the less lonely you are." And it's not difficult to see why, he continues: "Lack of trust makes you wary in your contact with others. If you can't open up to the other person, it prevents a connection from forming. Thus, distrust has an isolating effect."

YOUR OWN CONVOY

Being kinder with the people around you (and yourself), opening up to others, practicing your social skills—all of these things can help you connect more with people around you. Because, as Olivia Laing writes, "the lonelier you are, the less adept you become at navigating the currents of social intercourse." Cognitive behavioral therapy (CBT) can help, too, by teaching you to interpret your own negative thoughts differently. Research shows that when you feel lonely, your normal awareness of social cues can change into an exaggerated alertness to social cues and "social dangers." For example, if you don't succeed in chatting with someone at a party, someone who is lonely can be too inclined to think *nobody likes me*. Mindfulness training can help you refocus.

Preventing loneliness is easier than remedying it once it has developed. Jenny Gierveld refers to this as maintaining your "social convoy." "There is a lot that can be done to combat loneliness," she writes, "but the primary responsibility lies with ourselves: it's really up to each of us to build and maintain a convoy of people." Because "just as a convoy of ships is better protected against attacks by pirates, a convoy of people is more resistant to the risks of loneliness." Keeping up with your relationships takes time and energy, but "when loneliness comes knocking on your door, for whatever reason, there will be people around you who know you and who want to help you." And

you'll be there, ready to offer support to your convoy companions, too.

KNOW YOURSELF

I find Gierveld's advice clear but also challenging. Mostly because, as an introvert, I'm not sure if that convoy of mine is all sorted. For a long time I have felt like I should be making more friends—organizing more dinners, more nights out, more activities with friends. But in the meantime, I've also gotten to know myself better and I know now that a very social style of convoy doesn't suit me. I have a relationship that I am very happy in, and I have a small group of good friends with whom I share a strong emotional connection—but I don't, for instance, have groups of friends who regularly go out or go on vacation together. These trips look so idyllic in advertisements and on social media, but to be honest, I don't crave that. I'm a rather quiet person, and it doesn't make me lonely.

> **"Loneliness is the human condition. Cultivate it. The way it tunnels into you allows your soul room to grow."**
>
> —Janet Fitch, American author

Journalist Liesbeth Smit writes that "it would be a misunderstanding to associate loneliness with introverts. Enjoying time alone is not the same as being lonely, and being lonely certainly doesn't always go together with being alone. Charging up your batteries on your own is necessary for many introverts. But too much quietness can also eventually lead to feelings of being uprooted and dislodged." I relate to this. There are times when I work too much and get out of the house too little. I'll miss my children's school drop-off, and chats with other parents that I'd have on an otherwise socially quiet day.

ELDER LONELINESS

In 2016, 43 percent of the adult population (19 years and older) reported being lonely. But among those adults, professor of sociology Theo van Tilburg reports that the strongest feelings of loneliness occur among the elderly: "Their network is shrinking and meaningful contact with people they know becomes more and more rare." A loss of control over one's life—because of decreased mobility or other health factors—can intensify those feelings. But having a varied network can help: As you age, forge relationships outside of your family and intimate relationships, and keep in contact with neighbors and acquaintances.

It reminds me that I shouldn't forget to push myself to meet others, too. I could take a walk early in the morning with that nice neighbor, and we could drink coffee together on the stoop before before I go upstairs upstairs to my home office for another day's work.

The key to protecting myself against loneliness is, like most things, all in the balance. I will continue to try to cultivate a varied range of social relationships—as long as I remember to do it in a way that suits me. Gierveld agrees that it's worth checking in with yourself, because "some people want a lot of contacts, other people are more modest and would like a small group of contacts. Where one person may be content with one best friend, someone else might not find that sufficient: The higher you set the bar, the greater the chance that you will be lonely."

FEELING ALIVE

Another solution to loneliness advocated by philosopher Lars Svendsen is to learn to be alone, basically like I learned to be in the summer of 1991. Svendsen suggests that "loneliness is the dark side of being alone. But being alone can also lead to solitude: in solitude you are alone with yourself, in solitude you are together with yourself." Svendsen is convinced that many people, whether lonely or not, can't resist filling every empty moment of the day. It is that tendency to pick up the smartphone again and again whenever you're waiting in line, in a waiting room, during a train ride, during a break. This way you're not only depriving yourself of moments of quiet in which you can think, reflect, and come up with new ideas—you're also fanning that constant need to connect with others via social media.

It's also good to remember that it's a normal part of life to feel lonely every now and then. "It would be strange if you never felt lonely, because as a human being you need to have a connection with others. But at the same time, of course, it's not a need that can be filled every single moment of your life," Svendsen writes. It's a feeling that can hit you at a party when you don't know anyone and you can't join in a conversation. Or when you feel like going to the movies but nobody can go with you and you don't have it in you to simply go alone. That temporary lonely feeling can be healthy, though. I remember clearly how at the beginning of high school, my friendship with my best friend suddenly ended: I hadn't seen it coming and we didn't talk about it to each other. It just happened and I think we were too young to find words for our feelings. It was painful, and I remember how lost I felt without her. Fortunately, after a while, I managed to make new friends again, but it also helped me realize that, for me, one friendship is not enough.

Laing eventually started feeling less lonely again, too. Not so much because she got to know new people, but she moved on through her experiences with art: "When I started to feel whole again, it was not because I had met someone or was in love, but because I was guided by things that others had made and through that contact I gradually realized that loneliness, desire, does not mean that you have failed, but simply that you are alive."

WANT TO READ MORE?
- *The Lonely City: On the Art of Being Alone* by Olivia Laing

- *A Philosophy of Loneliness* by Lars Svendsen

ME, MYSELF, AND I

══ BY EVA LOESBERG ══

Twenty-four hours in nature, alone.
No phone, no book, no food.
What impact can nature have when
we remove barriers and truly embrace it?

It's July 5. I set down my backpack between two trees by a small lake—or, more accurately, a large pond—somewhere in the middle of a forest. This is my home for the next twenty-four hours. Henrik, the supervisor of this nature quest, saves the GPS coordinates so that a ranger can find me in an emergency and then he leaves. I am on my own now. I look at the green water in the pond. For weeks, I have been fantasizing about this moment, with all those empty hours ahead of me. How would I feel sitting still, something I never do. There is always a plan to be made, some weeding to do, someone to email, a kid who wants to play a game or learn to ride a bike. Maybe that's what appealed to me about the nature quest: how radically different it will be for me to remove all those distractions. Here, there's just me and nature. No food, no Netflix, no messaging, no magazines. I love the idea. And I'm petrified. Will I be able to stand the silence, the boredom? And what about wild animals?

Rijk Smitskamp, the founder of this nature quest, was far from reassuring during the introduction meeting. "The whole point is to be confronted with your fears to overcome them," he said. "An outdoor nature quest is meant to push you to the edges of your comfort zone. It might be cold, it might rain, there may be animals, you might not sleep. But what you then take back with you into your daily life is the sense that you have overcome all of this. You have yourself and that's all you need. You can feel confident that you'll make the right choices."

IMPROVISED TENT

I've been given a tent cloth for shelter, a whistle, and a tarp to lie on. My own packing list was short: a sleeping bag, a mat, warm clothes, toilet paper, a shovel to dig a hole for a toilet, a flashlight, two bottles of water (one mixed with lemon juice and maple syrup), mosquito repellent, tick tweezers, and a hat. That's it.

Just like at home, I immediately make a plan. First, I'll hang up the tent cloth, then make my bed and establish the circle Henrik described: "If you want to take on the challenge," he said, "make a circle with a diameter of four meters and stay inside it. You will find everything you need there." Namely, yourself. Like a woman possessed, I get started. I choose two trees, stretch the ropes, remove thistles, pull off protruding leaves, and unfold the groundsheet. But I am still not satisfied. I switch trees and move everything around until it feels right.

I like the idea that five other "questers" in the same forest are setting up their camps at this same moment. I met them for the first time this morning. We are each alone, but in this together.

Once I've put the mat and sleeping bag under the tarp, my residence for the night is ready. I make a circle out of branches, and am quickly able to settle in. That's when I feel like it's really started. The sun is high. I have hours and hours to go. I reassure myself that if I don't manage to keep sitting here, I'll just walk around and, in twenty-four hours, it will be over and I can check the nature quest off my to-do list.

The silence I had been expecting doesn't actually exist at all.

Only when the whinnying dies away in the distance do I dare to breathe again, and get up.

CRICKETS, DRAGONFLIES, AND BEES

I feel a gentle breeze. The leaves of the large tree are rustling. An intense fatigue overwhelms me. I lie down in the circle, watching the passing clouds—not fluffy sheep, but wisps, like the smoke from a chimney. I suddenly hear birds singing and chirping, as if they've just arrived. It's the same with the buzzing bees, which are hopping from flower to flower in my circle and flying out again. Chirping crickets are hiding in the tall grass. The silence I had been expecting doesn't actually exist at all. *Splash*—something jumps in the water. Two dragonflies skim over it. There is so much to be heard and seen. A line of ants marches past. Some walk around the tall blades of grass; others over them. "Hey guys, there is a better way to get there," I think out loud, because nobody can hear me anyway. But what does it matter how long they take? And who says the shortest route is the best?

Proudly, I think: *I can do this*. How could I have ever thought I'd be bored? Nature is moving all the time. Once you've adjusted to the slower rhythm, time flies. The sun disappears from my circle and sinks behind the tall trees. What is it about nature?

According to Dutch scientific journalist Mark Mieras, there is increasing evidence that the stress-reducing effect of nature comes from phytoncides, a substance that plants and trees secrete to protect themselves against insects. When we inhale these, they wake up our immune system and the stress hormone level in our body drops. Another explanation is that when we come into contact with soil bacteria that we have evolved with in tandem, they cause serotonin to be released in our brains.

NIGHTTIME

Whatever the explanation, I feel cheerful and calm. I am hungry, though. But the fasting during this quest has a reason. "Eating has become a [mindless] habit in our society," Rijk said. "We put all kinds of food in our mouth without thinking about it, and it's good to become aware of that." I notice that not eating gives me a floating sensation, which makes the conversations I'm having in my head with family and friends have a sentimental effect on me.

It's getting cooler. "Make sure that you enter your sleeping bag when you're still warm," Henrik had said, so I take off my shoes to put on thicker socks and am promptly bitten under my foot by a horsefly, which I then fight with for a while because it would like to bite me again. I'm on guard. Night falls. I feel secure in my spot, as if the trees, whose leaf clusters I can now trace from memory, are protecting me. Also, I have a whistle. My only concerns now are foxes, snakes, mice, or rats coming under my tarp. And then there are those giant wild horses that we saw during the walk that I've heard neighing in the distance. . . .

Snugly tucked in, I lie on my mat listening to the rustling in the bushes. As if I can keep the animals at bay with my ears. And then, when I least expect it, I fall into a deep sleep. When I wake up, dawn is breaking. I'm guessing it's around 5 a.m. I hear hooves. My mat vibrates. The horses! Carefully, I push the cloth aside and see three colossal beasts standing by the pond a few meters away. I can hear them gulping water and snorting. They are such powerful animals. If only I had a camera, I think, as the first rays of the sun frame them in halos. The brown one seems impatient, or maybe playful. It runs back and forth across the sand. Please don't run into my tarp, I think with my heart pounding. Only when the whinnying dies away in the distance do I dare to breathe again, and get up.

NO MORE LISTS

The sun still has to rise much higher before Henrik will pick me up around noon. I long for my family, food, a chair to sit on—the ground is very hard, after all—but at the same time I don't want to leave. The peace that I feel is almost intoxicating. I don't remember ever feeling this way before. And it didn't take any effort. I'm already making a resolution to spend much more time outdoors. According to researchers from Nippon Medical School in Tokyo, a three-hour nature walk can have calming effects on the mind and body that last for a whole week.

Back at base camp, we eat lentil soup and share our experiences. Some of us found it harder than others, but we all agree that this natural environment, which has such a magical effect on us, should be cherished more lovingly.

Two days later, I still feel a lightness. Everything seems to be simpler and easier with nature's aftereffects still lingering. Not only did I check off the nature quest from my to-do list, I've deleted my to-do list. We'll see what happens. And how long I can hold on to this peacefulness within me.

Befriend a Book

A book is a friend at whose doorstep
you can show up unannounced with a
fresh thermos of tea. And with one of these
bookmarks, you can always easily pick up
the "conversation" right where you left off,
as if no time has passed between you.

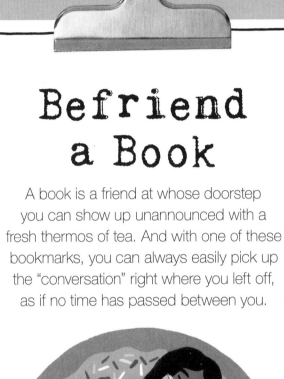

A BOOK IS A DREAM YOU CAN HOLD IN YOUR HANDS.

NEIL GAIMAN

flow workman

ILLUSTRATION
HOLLY MAGUIRE

IF YOU ONLY READ THE BOOKS THAT EVERYONE ELSE IS READING, YOU CAN ONLY THINK WHAT EVERYONE ELSE IS THINKING.

HARUKI MURAKAMI

flow workman

ILLUSTRATION
SANNY VAN LOON

BOOKS ARE UNIQUELY PORTABLE MAGIC.

STEPHEN KING

flow workman

ILLUSTRATION
YELENA BRYKSENKOVA

BOOKS MAKE PEOPLE QUIET. YET THEY ARE SO LOUD.

NNEDI OKORAFOR

flow workman

ILLUSTRATION
SANNY VAN LOON

HOW DO YOU KEEP GOING WHEN YOU'RE GRIEVING?

BY ANNEMIEK LECLAIRE

We each deal with grief in our own personal way. Here, a journalist mourns the loss of her partner and wonders if there are any universal answers for how she can cope with her immense grief.

Mourning, whatever the loss
that causes it, is as
personal as a fingerprint.

"Never forget that I love you very, very much." Those were the last words my beloved said to me. He was going on vacation and I had dropped by to say goodbye. He had put his hands on my face and looked me in the eyes. Such an intense declaration wasn't rare, so I couldn't really work out why I was so anxious as I rode home that afternoon. He was healthy, athletic, and strong. Still, when I didn't get a reply to my message the next morning, I wrote in my diary, "I'm so worried my stomach hurts. Was this gift of love only possible as a last moment before death?" Was it fear or intuition? He was already dead when I wrote it.

LOTS TO LOSE

We all have to deal with overwhelming loss in our lives. According to Flemish psychologist and mourning specialist Manu Keirse, when it comes to mourning, people primarily think of the reactions after a death, but the concept is much broader. He says that it is the human response to any form of loss: being diagnosed with a serious illness, being fired, failing at school, a relationship ending, and even the loss of an important belief.

Keirse believes some losses are often not recognized as losses: children and parents who are estranged, grandparents who don't see their grandkids, life with an alcoholic partner. "Something can die inside you that nobody sees," says Keirse. "You're mourning something that you have never been able to process, because you have never been allowed or able to express it. Or because your grieving process is not recognized by others."

When I got divorced, I felt like I had fallen off a cliff. I likened the grief of breaking up to the pain I experienced giving birth: I knew I could bear it, but I still had to ride it out.

Mourning, whatever the loss that causes it, is as personal as a fingerprint. That in itself is comforting. Nevertheless, experts say there are a few general guidelines to finding a healthy path through the grief. The first one is "experiencing the reality of the loss." As I write this, just a few months after the death of my loved one, I find it difficult to realize that he is gone forever. As that awareness deepens, the pain also grows. "That [awareness] can take a long time," Keirse says. "Your heart is not ready, your brain is numb."

"Accepting that pain" is the second guideline. American author Elizabeth Gilbert, who lost her partner to cancer, describes her grief as a wave that washes over at unexpected times: "[It] has its own timeframe, it has its own itinerary with you, it has its own power over you, and it will come when it comes . . . in the middle of the night, comes in the middle of the day, comes in the middle of a meeting, comes in the middle of a meal." Resistance isn't just futile, she asserts, it can be even more painful. Because when "it arrives—it's this tremendously forceful arrival and . . . to stiffen, to resist, and to fight it is to hurt yourself."

SUPPORT

New Zealand author Dr. Lucy Hone says that acceptance of the loss and of the feelings that are unleashed is essential. An expert in resilience and well-being, Hone was a consultant during the earthquakes that besieged New Zealand for two years, on how to deal with the loss of loved ones, homes, and businesses; the loss of certainty that the earth will not buckle

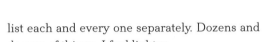

> **"I'm not lost for I know where I am. But however, where I am may be lost."**
>
> —A.A. Milne (1882-1956), in *Winnie-the-Pooh*

and shake everything. And then, in 2014, she lost her twelve-year-old in a car accident. "We were told it would take five years to get over her death," Hone says. "I didn't have five years. I had two sons, fourteen and sixteen, who needed me." Her new motto became: *Don't lose what you have to what you've already lost.* In her book *Resilient Grieving*, Hone explains the strategies that kept her going. She calls it pro-active mourning: restoring routines from before. "It gives the brain a signal," she says, "that chaos is over, and safety has returned." In her case, it meant breakfast with her children, walks with her dog, exercising, and going to work. What also helped her was a deep conviction that sadness is the inevitable flipside of a life lived in love.

POWERFUL ANTIDOTE

Being able to see the good things in life is another positive psychology strategy that helps re-establish control in life. On a cold Saturday evening I walk through the city alone. Behind the windows I see lights, families, people together. Thousands of people in the city and not one of them is him. With every step, I count my blessings: my beautiful son, one. My beautiful daughter, two. My healthy parents, three and four. My family, my friends, my clients, my work, my safe home, my able body, the books on my shelves, the lake nearby, the sounds of the market on Saturday mornings, the florist . . . I

list each and every one separately. Dozens and dozens of things. I feel lighter.

According to Keirse, this realization that you can take action is a powerful antidote to the powerlessness that you experience when you're grieving. He calls this mourning work. "It explains," he says, "why sad people can some-times be so tired."

The first week after the death of my loved one I spent my days in nature. I sat by the lake and watched the clouds. There was a rising chill in the air, the birds flew overhead. It calmed me to be able to sit and think about his last moments and wonder what his last wish would be, if there was anything else I could do for him, and what he would have said I should do now. I had lost my most important ally, and also my perspective on the future. "A story has been cut short," says Keirse, while Hone advises: "Be at ease; silence and inwardness are needed to make you under-stand what the loss means and to slowly develop a new story."

A miscarriage, a child who is self-destruc-tive, a toxic relationship from which you cannot escape: Whatever causes the sorrow, it creates loneliness. Keirse believes in the importance of supporting each other; of people learning a lit-tle more about how we can help one another, because if we don't feel at ease talking about sadness, people around us will sense it and hide their feelings.

BEAR WITNESS TO SADNESS

Connection has been scientifically proven to provide relief from sadness. In her book *Option B*, author Sheryl Sandberg identifies people she calls "openers"—or people who dare to call mourning by its name. People who don't dare mention it, or who are judgmental, are what I call "loneliness doublers"—they often show up with well-intended but hurtful statements. Keirse is familiar with the scenario. If your child dies at birth, it goes like this, *You're still young. You can have another one.* If your mother dies in old age, *You can be happy that you were able to know her for so long.* "Instead, one should try to bear witness to someone's sadness instead of trying to determine its purpose," he says. Bearing witness means "more observing than doing, more listening than talking, and more following than leading. This is how you confirm the dignity and authority of the person feeling the sorrow."

It reminds me of what British poet David Whyte writes about friendship in his book *Consolations*. "The ultimate touchstone of friendship is . . . witness, the privilege of having been seen by someone and the equal privilege of being granted the sight of the essence of another, to have walked with them and to have believed in them, and sometimes just to have accompanied them for however brief a span, on a journey impossible to accomplish alone."

SPECKS OF LIGHT

My love had such an appreciation for the smallest things in life. That appreciation now carries me further: Despite the pain or perhaps thanks to it, I see the moon in the sky, the water smooth like glass, the roses that climb the wall of his house. It is amazing how many specks of light become visible when darkness falls.

WANT TO READ MORE?

- *Resilient Grieving: Finding Strength and Embracing Life After a Loss That Changes Everything* by Lucy Hone

- *Option B: Facing Adversity, Building Resilience, and Finding Joy* by Sheryl Sandberg and Adam Grant

- *Consolations: The Solace, Nourishment and Underlying Meaning of Everyday Words* by David Whyte

═══ BY CARINE DE KOONING ═══

*What's the best way to adjust to life on your own
when a romantic relationship comes to an end?
Here are some collected tips from experts and friends.*

It was the last Friday before the Christmas holiday. I came home and my son was at a party, my daughter was at a sleepover, and my husband had gone out with his buddies. Instead of looking forward to our usual Friday evening ritual—family movie on the couch—I parked my bicycle next to the empty house, and felt completely disoriented by the force of the solitude. This is my future, I thought, because my husband and I were divorcing in January. I cried uncontrollably on the couch.

THE LITTLE BLEEP OF SALVATION

That evening is etched in my memory as the first time I was really alone. I hated it so much that I scheduled something for every minute that I would be without my family over the forthcoming weeks. Yoga, dinners out, a movie and, if I had nothing else going on, I took my laptop to the study hall of the nearby university just so that I wasn't alone. I didn't know anyone there, but I felt uplifted by the communal energy.

But then came a Friday where I had nothing planned. As the evening loomed closer, I felt a rising panic and sent a message out to all my friends at once. I confessed my desperate need for company to a friend who was very experienced at being alone. She replied with this advice: "You have to engage with the pain. You have to work your way through it. These evenings are inescapable and very important."

I knew she was right *and* I was enormously relieved when my phone beeped again, and I had an invitation to join another friend at the movies. The thing I used to fantasize about when my children were small (just one day on my own!) turned out to be too much to handle. Maybe, in the end, being alone is only desirable in the midst of activity.

TURBULENT WATERS

Why is being alone so hard for many people? According to Dutch psychology professor Nele Jacobs, the pain of loneliness is a drive to action. "Hunger and tiredness can be difficult to endure," she explains, "but hunger drives us to eat and tiredness drives us to sleep. In the same way, the discomfort of being alone drives us to seek out social contact."

So it's not surprising that I'm doing everything I can to avoid the pain of being alone. The sadness stays with me anyway, sometimes surging at unexpected moments. In the middle of a conversation, waves of emotion wash over me and I surface again gasping for air. I'm alive, but still I need to learn to swim better in the turbulent and unpredictable sea of loneliness.

Loneliness doesn't necessarily require physical solitude, but rather an absence of connection, closeness, kinship.

ALONE BY CHOICE

The number of single-person households around the world is rising. And, according to Dutch trendwatcher Lieke Lamb, this is not just because of ageing populations and of divorces. "Women are more highly educated," says Lamb, "and an increasingly large part of that demographic prefers to go solo instead of leading a traditional life with a partner and children."

Lamb expects that, especially with ever-advancing technologies, living alone will continue to become easier for the elderly, too. "Apps help you arrange for individually tailored care, and it's also becoming possible to share equipment and access more support services," she says.

SENSE OF LOSS

But all of this technology isn't helping people feel less lousy about being alone. In her book *The Lonely City*, British author Olivia Laing writes about how she fared after moving from London to New York for love, and the relationship fell apart. "Cities can be lonely places," she writes, "and in admitting this we see that loneliness doesn't necessarily require physical solitude, but rather an absence of connection."

Loneliness is the negative side to being alone; it's an experience that involves missing someone so much that you can feel enormous frustration and even anger. Luckily, being alone doesn't *have* to mean feeling lonely. And,

like many other social skills, being alone is a skill that can be acquired.

SOCIAL CREATURES

Annemie Ploeger, assistant professor in developmental psychology at the University of Amsterdam, specializes in evolutionary psychology. "Some primates live in savannas and grasslands," she says. "During the transition from the woodlands to the plains, working together was incredibly important. We needed each other to survive, so humans developed as social animals."

Ploeger sees a link with chimpanzees, with whom we are genetically most closely related. "They are very social animals," she says. "They sleep together in a nest in a tree and their social structure has the same hierarchy as we adhere to in business or politics." From that perspective it's not all that strange that we don't like being alone. But according to Ploeger, it's not that simple. "We're also related to orangutans and these animals lead a solitary life and sleep alone," she says. "A male only hangs around a female during her fertile period."

We resemble chimpanzees more than orangutans, though, Ploeger says, so it's more likely that being alone is not a structural part of our DNA. But humans are also the most adaptive species on earth. "Our prefrontal cortex— the area in our brain that enables planning—is far more developed than in other primates," Ploeger says. "This helps us, for example, decide that we may not want to marry and have children; we may want to stay alone."

ADAPTATION

A good friend had been in a relationship for twenty years before he had to go it alone. "The first month was hell," he tells me. "I completely fell apart and didn't know how to get from one day to the next. Yet slowly but surely there were more and more days when things were going well. There were even hours here and there when I didn't think about my loss at all."

After three months, the initial shock passed, and he was managing to move forward. "At the beginning, I would fill every second of the day just to make sure I was never alone, but sometimes that just intensified my feelings of loneliness. I slowly learned to find my footing in being alone and began spacing out my appointments. If you invest in connections that really give you energy, these can compensate for the emptiness."

SURVIVAL STRATEGIES

Deep down I know that, some day, I'll have to accept being alone without any plans or get-togethers to distract me. Almost everyone who's been through this tells me it's been a valuable period in their life—in hindsight, of course. Everyone had their own strategy to get through. One tip I got is to find something that moves you. For some it's classical music or the-ater. I find it in books; I can feel truly consoled by beautiful writing.

A friend of mine who is a mindfulness trainer suggests: "When you're feeling really sad, it can help to talk to yourself like a loving mother talks to her child when it's sad. I tried it out and unbelievably, she's right: Conjuring up an imaginary mother who wraps her arms

around you when you're lying on the couch, crying, really does work.

Another friend told me, "At a certain moment you'll recognize this crappy feeling you're having and just think, *Oh there it is again*. By recognizing it and maybe even acknowledging it, you become used to it."

These mindful methods of pain management are affirmed by another friend, who says: "I used to feel so sorry for myself when the kids were with their dad on one of those empty Sundays. But I also enjoyed the peace and quiet, and read the entire newspaper uninterrupted."

I am terrible at being alone. I still feel like an absolute beginner, but I do know this much: This is a skill I don't want to develop to perfec-tion. I'm dreaming about a big plot of land with ten houses on it where I can live with all my dearest friends, and grow old peacefully—with a new partner as well. Because no matter how many opportunities possibly being alone brings, I am at *my* best when I'm with someone.

HOW TO:
MAKE DUTCH PANCAKES
(FROM SCRATCH)

1.

BASIC RECIPE: 1⅝ C FLOUR ✻ 1¼ C MILK ✻ 3 EGGS ✻ PINCH OF SALT ✻ BUTTER OR OIL

2. MIX YOUR BATTER IN STEPS: CRACK THE EGGS INTO THE MIXING BOWL AND BEAT THEM UNTIL THEY'RE SMOOTH. NEXT ADD THE MILK TO THE EGGS AND MIX WELL. ADD THE FLOUR BIT BY BIT AND KEEP WHISKING. DON'T FORGET THE PINCH OF SALT.

3. SOME PEOPLE SAY ADDING A SPLASH OF BEER TO THE BATTER IS THEIR SECRET INGREDIENT: IT GIVES THE PANCAKES A LOVELY CRUNCHINESS. (SPRITE WORKS, TOO.)

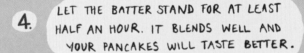

4. LET THE BATTER STAND FOR AT LEAST HALF AN HOUR. IT BLENDS WELL AND YOUR PANCAKES WILL TASTE BETTER.

5. THAT STORY ABOUT THE FIRST PANCAKE ALWAYS FAILING IS A FABLE: IT JUST MEANS THE PAN WASN'T HOT ENOUGH YET. GIVE IT TIME TO GET PROPERLY HOT.

7.

POUR THE BATTER IN THE PAN WITH A SOUP LADLE AND SWIRL THE BATTER AROUND THE PAN EVENLY. LET IT COOK FOR ABOUT THREE MINUTES UNTIL THE TOP IS DRY.

6.

PUT BUTTER OR OIL IN THE PAN AND MAKE SURE IT COVERS THE PAN ENTIRELY SO YOUR PANCAKE DOESN'T STICK. OIL IS HEALTHIER, BUTTER MAKES PANCAKES GOLDEN BROWN.

9.

BOTH SIDES GOLDEN BROWN? READY TO EAT!

8.

FIRST LOOSEN THE PANCAKE A BIT BY SHAKING THE PAN A LITTLE. TURN IT OVER WITH A SPATULA AND BROWN THE OTHER SIDE OF THE PANCAKE FOR ABOUT ONE MINUTE ON MEDIUM HEAT. OR FLIP YOUR PANCAKE IN THE AIR (PRACTICE MAKES PERFECT).

TAKE YOURSELF ON A TRIP

BY ILSE SAVENIJE

It may take a few vacations to realize it, but it's important to remember that wherever you travel, you always take yourself with you. (And the challenges you face at home are not any easier to solve when you're away.)

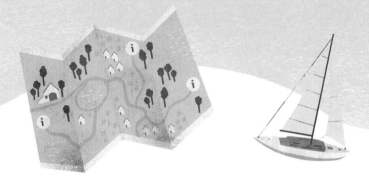

When things aren't going swimmingly at home, my automatic reaction is to go away on a trip. Just take a complete break from everything. Leave everything behind: the people, the apps, the work, my own self. Dreaming of a long vacation, I'm convinced that, away from home and distracted by adventure, I'll feel less stressed or sad. After all, when you go somewhere different, everything is new and full of experiences and fun, extroverted people—leading to a more carefree me.

But that's not how it plays out. I've had to experience several times now that all my thoughts and tendencies are packed in my backpack, too, especially during longer periods on the road. For example, during the first few weeks of a six-month internship in Sydney, Australia, I felt euphoric. But for the rest of my stay there I noticed that here I am sometimes tied up in my feelings and, just like at home, I don't know what to do when I feel unsure or sad. To recognize that felt disappointing.

A few years later, backpacking my way through South America, it happened again. There, too, while also enjoying days of hiking in groups and lovely afternoons on palm beaches, I was prone to worrying about what others thought of me and restless at the thought of "what's next." How annoying that my "old self" had joined me on this adventure once again.

At the same time, I realize how useful it is that that self travels with me. Because, despite my tendency to worry and overthink, I know I'll be able to manage if the hostel for the next night suddenly turns out to be full, or if the internet's not working in one of my temporary residences. And, if there's no one to swim with, I'll just have fun on my own. Because my

Distance brings perspective. You may see people living in different ways than you do. More minimalist, perhaps. Or more close to nature.

"old self" wasn't old or left behind. It was me. And as long as I'm there, I'll be fine.

TRAVEL AS AN ESCAPE

Why is this fallacy of thinking I can leave myself at home when I travel is so persistent? I asked psychologist Amy van den Broeck. Because she carries out her work as a digital nomad herself, offering remote support to travelers all over the world, she knows well the struggles and pitfalls of being on the move. At first glance, travelers' problems don't sound that different from those that many people face at home: anxiety, stress, feeling down. But also, there's homesickness and difficulty building relationships. When I tell her about my recurring challenge—that I keep thinking I can leave my "self" at home when I travel—she immediately confirms that many people see traveling as an escape. "We often glorify faraway destinations, thinking that our struggles will fall away from us there. And sometimes it works for a short while, because we're swept

There is no old me to leave at home and no new me somewhere faraway.

along in fun activities. But when it bubbles back up that you are still there in full, your problems come back."

ACCEPT YOUR STRUGGLES

Van den Broeck shares with me the mechanism behind it: avoidance behavior. "The fact that we want to avoid pain or fear is a biological reaction. In ancient times when primitive humans saw a bear, they had to fight or physically flee. Today, our fears tend to be more psychological. But uncomfortable or painful situations will always be part of our lives." She gives the example of a breakup: "When we're going through heartbreak, we want to feel good as soon as we can, and because a short-term reward is attractive, leaving town is an easy way out. By placing ourselves in a different context, we think we won't have to deal with our misery for a while."

I recognize myself in that scenario, in the appeal of leaving those worries at home. But it seems to actually work to lose the fear, stress, or sadness when you are distracted by sun and adventures on vacation, at least for a little while. So what about that? "It often does indeed work for a short period of time," she reports. "But in the long run, your struggles will always come back."

Van den Broeck also considers that we, as a society, have a low tolerance when it comes to problems. Bad luck, tension, boredom: We seem unable to accept that these things are a normal part of life. Social media, which often features only the fun and good times—plus a big helping of happy vacation photos—contributes to this. We don't witness much sadness in the online lives of others, so we start thinking that it's unnatural. Van den Broeck has had her own experiences with carrying problems around. "Everyone has a certain vulnerability. For me it's a tendency to feel gloomy and have negative thoughts. For many travelers, this vulnerability comes to light despite—or sometimes because of—being in a different environment. When you travel, your social network is often small, and because social support is so

important in life, you can quickly feel lonely or uprooted while away from home."

TO THE HEART OF THINGS

But Van den Broeck remains very positive about traveling. "I think it can spark wonderful changes," she says. "Especially on longer journeys—you can really get to the heart of things, and have the time to think in depth. Moreover, distance brings perspective. You may see people living in different ways than you do. More minimalist, perhaps. Or more close to nature. As a close-knit community, together with family and friends." A change in perspective can help you realize that you are capable of change. These opportunities for newness are still my main motive for packing my bags. Examining those motives is important, says Van den Broeck. Do you want to leave out of curiosity? Or do you feel bad, or bored? "In the case of the latter, you can try to change the way you look at things now. You can learn to tolerate certain emotions more, or deal with them differently. Another important point is getting to know your values, and working toward how you want to live, no matter where you are." Someone who feels lonely—at home or while traveling—can learn to allow themselves to feel alone at times. And then see how to get more togetherness in their life, too.

RIGHT BACK AT HOME

All in all, I really learned a lot during those vacations when I ran into that wall of my self. I now can identify more quickly when I actually should put my travel plans on pause for a while, even when it seems like the perfect escape at first. There is no old me to leave at home and no new me somewhere far away. So now when I think, *I'm stressed, I have to get out of here,* I don't necessarily reach for my backpack. But I definitely reach for it when I feel like hiking on a mountain or experiencing a different culture or a different speed of life. I've also learned that, for me, sometimes a few weeks away is enough. And I can take on the daily struggles again afterward. Right back at home.

As long as I'm there, I'll be fine.

Chapter 4

LOVE YOUR UNIQUE MIND

WHERE DID THE NOTION THAT WE SHOULD be able to do absolutely everything come from? We watch in awe as people we know preside over business meetings, give presentations, raise children, do yoga twice a week, and organize kid birthday parties that start in the afternoon and last through to the following morning. We're just not able to.

We once read something that has now become our mantra: Just do as much as you can. When you keep that in mind, life becomes simpler. It doesn't mean we're lazy. We have successful careers. We're very ambitious. But we avoid excesses and feel free enough to say when we can't do something. Instead, we do what we can.

Sometimes we spend an afternoon on the couch reading a book, even when the house is a mess. Sometimes we do something at work that's not perfect, but is good enough. Sometimes we say no to volunteering with the kids' sports team because we just can't. And we don't mind acknowledging that we're not good at some things, like baking cakes (Irene), using a sewing machine (Astrid), remembering birthdays and wrapping gifts nicely (Irene), or mingling at parties (Astrid).

The fact is, it's okay to admit you can't do something. It's a relief even. We're all uniquely qualified to do different things—the trick is to surround yourself with people who are good at doing the things you can't do.

THE BEAUTY OF STUMBLING

BY CAROLINE BUIJS

*As much as we prefer to forget those moments when we mess up,
reflecting on them can be very good for us and insightful.*

As a child, when I looked down at my legs, I was often greeted by two scraped knees. Tripping was as much a part of my childhood as the blackbird's song is part of spring. It was only later that my stumbling became embarrassing: in high school, when I tripped on my long scarf right in front of the boy I had a crush on. Or, when I was a newly arrived student in Amsterdam and my bicycle tire got stuck in a tram rail, causing me to fall down in the middle of a busy shopping street.

STOP FOR A MOMENT

Stumbling and falling are not only part of childhood—they are part of adulthood, too, though not always in the literal sense. Stumbling can mean not passing your exam, having your heart broken, or discovering that a new project you've taken on just isn't working out. It can be choosing a university major and, after you've started, finding out it doesn't suit you or snapping at your children just before they leave for school, and feeling bad about it all day. Stumbling is simply part of daily life, and with a bit of luck you learn something from it.

Stumbling forces us to stand still for a moment and think about why something didn't go well. It's too bad, really, that we generally avoid that moment of reflection, preferring instead to move on from our stumbles as quickly as possible. More often than we realize, this is because we are embarrassed. We'd rather avoid talking about our stumble with anyone. Sometimes we lash out at the people closest to us. As Dutch psychologist Arjan van Dam explains, when we are children we don't feel any embarrassment about tripping, because we don't have any insecurities about what the world thinks about us yet. It's only as we get older that we realize other people are watching us and judging us—that's when feelings of embarrassment start to surface. Imagine, says Van Dam, that you're living on a desert island with no people: Would you feel embarrassed if you stumbled there?

As American professor, author, and speaker Brené Brown writes in her book *Rising Strong*, a lot of people have this reaction when things don't go well: It's fight or flight, an age-old evolutionary impulse of our brain. But Brown's research also shows that the most resilient people have a different approach: They are not afraid of uncomfortable feelings, so instead of fighting or fleeing, they stand still. They obscure their feelings and consider the ways in which their feelings are connected to their thoughts and behavior.

THAT OLD STORY AGAIN

In her book, Brown writes that when we stumble or fall, we tell ourselves stories to make sense of the hurt it creates—the anger, frustration or pain. ". . . Our minds go to work trying to make sense of what's happening," she writes. "The story is driven by emotion and the immediate need to self-protect, which means it's most likely not accurate, well thought out, or even civil."

That is wholly understandable. As American neurologist and novelist Robert Burton explains, our brain rewards us with dopamine when we recognize and complete a pattern. Stories are patterns, with a beginning, a middle, and an end. "Because we feel compelled to think of stories," Burton says, "we are often forced to accept an incomplete story and make it work somehow."

We all have some story or another at the ready that we've developed in the course of our lifetimes and have come to believe in. I myself often resort to the "they probably think I am stupid" story. And I escape my fear of being seen as stupid by fleeing. I had a pretty bad stumble in my life, when I started work as a teacher. It took me just one week to find out that actually teaching *really* didn't suit me at all. I was embarrassed, because the simple truth was I didn't know how to manage a classroom full of kids. My response was to quit my job a mere four weeks in, telling everyone that it was a bad school, that I wasn't given any guidance, and that the teaching materials were of poor quality. Instead of thinking it over and reflecting on any lessons I could have learned from this experience, I switched course and took a job at a travel agency. It wasn't the job of my dreams, but I felt I could do it well without stumbling again.

EMBRACING OUR STUMBLES

What if we could embrace our falls, and see them as opportunities to learn? Van Dam suggests that it's actually kind of silly that we think it's okay for little kids to make mistakes but not

Action almost never
leads to regret
in the long term.

adults. "I find it very suffocating to think that we should be able to do everything faultlessly all the time," he says. "Maybe it's fed by social media, where people only show how well they're doing. A person's value nowadays sometimes seems determined by what they have achieved."

Van Dam says it can be helpful to let go of the idea that we have arrived. It's better to think we are "becoming" and therefore, like a child, we need space to develop. "It's more important than ever now," Van Dam says. "The world is changing so fast, and it's hard to adapt if you don't keep developing yourself."

What also helps, he says, is to understand how irrational it is to never allow for some stumbling. "I think your life will be more fun if your basic outlook is that mistakes help you learn," he says. "Or that stumbling helps you learn. A friend of mine would often joke, 'You get to make one mistake in life.' I used that line for a while; once the cheesemonger at a market started laughing right away and replied, 'No

way, man, then you'd never learn a thing, would you.' So try that: Tell yourself you get to make only one mistake in life, so you can just hear how illogical it is . . . it just doesn't make sense to live that way.

FAILURE IS PROGRESS

What really helped me after my teaching debacle was to read a lot and watch lots of movies, because almost every novel or movie has a main character who needs to overcome setbacks. It can be comforting, because you get to see someone succeed—or not, and then you get an idea of how to go about things.

In his book *Black Box Thinking*, British author Matthew Syed explains why some people learn from their mistakes and others don't. The difference depends on how we view our mistakes, he says. People who are of the opinion that they can become smarter from dedication and perseverance view mistakes differently than people who tend to believe that their basic characteristics, such as intelligence or talents, are largely fixed. "Because they believe that progress is driven, in large part, by practice," Syed writes, "they naturally regard failure as an inevitable aspect of learning. . . . Those who think that success emerges from talent and innate intelligence, on the other hand, are far more likely to be threatened by their mistakes. They will regard failures as evidence that they don't have what it takes, and never will; after all, you can't change what you were born with. They are going to be far more intimidated by situations in which they will be judged. Failure is dissonant."

NOT YET

In her 2014 TED Talk, American psychology professor Carol Dweck discusses the power of

Imagine if you lived on a desert island with no people: Would you feel embarrassed if you stumbled there?

the words "not yet." At a school in Chicago, instead of students' exams being graded a "fail," they were marked with the result "not yet." As Dweck explains, this helped to remind the students that they were in a learning process, as opposed to a fail grade that made many students feel they didn't amount to anything. Dweck says you can encourage the intention of "not yet" by, for example, no longer praising intelligence or talent, but focusing more on attitude and effort.

The idea that stumbling is a bad thing is a dangerous one because you might then live your life overly cautiously to ensure you never trip up. You just stay put wherever you are. (Or you keep working, as I did, at a travel agency because it's nice and safe, while deep down you know that you want to do something else.) What may help is to know that maybe you'll regret doing something more than not doing it in the short term, but in the long term it works the other way around. Dutch psychologist Ap Dijksterhuis explains that we are sometimes afraid to make decisions that lead to insecure situations. He writes that because we're sometimes faced with regret after making a choice to do something, we think, often subconsciously, that we'd best act cautiously by delaying or canceling plans. Yet when it comes to the really

important big decisions—and therefore the risk of real, big, and long-term regret—it is precisely this lack of action that fails us. According to Dijksterhuis, action almost never leads to regret in the long term.

Dijksterhuis also writes about researchers who interviewed a large group of elderly people on what they regretted most when looking back on their lives. Four times as many people mentioned something they didn't do and now felt they should have done—inaction—than the number of people who regretted doing something that maybe they shouldn't have. In other words, sometimes you've got to be brave, and simply accept the risk that's involved if you stumble. As Dutch artist and adventurer Joost Conijn writes: "When you know too much in advance, there are countless reasons not to."

EMPATHY AS AN ANTIDOTE

That still leaves the question: What can we do with that sense of embarrassment when we stumble? In one of her TED Talks, Brown says that embarrassment needs three things to grow extreme: secrecy, silence, and judgment. Luckily there is also an antidote to embarrassment, and that's empathy. Ask for help when you fall. Be kind to yourself. Think, as Brown herself does, every morning when you wake up: It doesn't matter what I manage and what I don't—I am good enough. And instead of getting mad at yourself or feeling like a loser, just say the words, "not yet."

WANT TO READ MORE?
- *Rising Strong* by Brené Brown
- *Black Box Thinking: The Surprising Truth About Success* by Matthew Syed

THE IMPORTANCE TRAP

BY FLEUR BAXMEIER

*Why do we always put off the big, important tasks
and tackle the little things first? Is there a better way
to approach all the things we need to do?*

Thirteen years ago, when I went to view the house where I now live, my first thought was, "It's perfect, but the metal kitchen cabinets have to go. I need to get rid of those rickety cupboards, the old oven, the moldy drain, and the leaky refrigerator." Those were only the first things I planned to do.

The only stumbling block was that, as a freelancer, it seemed impossible to find a time when all the work could be done. Preferably not during a really busy period, but how do you plan for *that*? Finding the right contractor was another problem. Next, my boyfriend and I couldn't agree on the color palette.

Years passed, and I thought about that unrealized new kitchen often. Every evening as I would prepare yet another meal on the two burners that still worked. Eventually, the need to make major changes to my open-plan kitchen—visible from every corner of the ground floor—became an excuse to put off making other changes to my home's interior.

I'LL JUST SEND THIS EMAIL FIRST . . .

The new-kitchen-that-never-materialized had a paralyzing effect on everything. It is a common phenomenon referred to as the "Importance Trap." Paul Loomans, Dutch Zen monk and the author of *Time Surfing*, says, "The Importance Trap is about all those tasks that are so important to us that we wait until all the conditions are just right before we tackle them. But we wind up in a sort of stalemate, even though we are constantly thinking how we need to just do it."

Putting off the important things has to do with the times we live in, when information is coming at us in small increments and at great speed. Take emails, for example. They send constant additions to our to-do lists, and there are always a few that require prompt attention. "If your focus is on these smaller tasks, you'll never get around to completing that one large one," Loomans says. "This is why it's important to be proactive instead of reactive. Suppose you get up in the morning and you want to do your paperwork today, but you open your email inbox first instead. At this point, you're taking a reactive approach, because the emails are flooding in. Responses to your responses then start coming in, so you stay where you are, driven only by what is coming into your inbox."

A proactive approach means that, before you open up your emails, you think about what you really want to do that day. "This is something that we should not only do in the morning, but maybe even six times each day," says Loomans. "Step back from what you're doing . . . Then you can see the big picture, and from there choose your next move."

RAPID REWARDS

In an ideal world, a proactive attitude would help us complete any significant task that we want. In reality, however, we're wired to crave short-term happiness—the instant shot of satisfaction we get from completing a small, simple task like replying to an email or posting a photo on social media. Bigger jobs don't deliver that same quick dose of dopamine, so we have to make a conscious choice to do them. Canadian American author and speaker Brian Tracy calls prioritizing key tasks and doing them first "eating the frog."

"Your 'frog' is your biggest, most important task, the one you are most likely to procrastinate on if you don't do something about it," he writes in his book *Eat That Frog*. He encourages developing a routine in which you eat your frog before you do anything else.

But when it comes to the long-term projects like writing a book, learning a language, or even just clearing out a bedroom—the sheer scale of the task can be daunting. It feels like too much to wrap our heads around, so we ignore it and tell ourselves we'll return to it later. Meanwhile, that undone task hovers in the back of our minds, quietly causing stress. American author and life coach Tony Robbins is an advocate of a technique he calls "chunking"—breaking the large task down into easy-to-achieve steps. "If you take on a project and try to do the whole thing all at once," he says, "you're going to be overwhelmed. And similarly, if you take a task and break it into too many small steps, it's equally overwhelming." He advises that by "taking all that is coming at you and putting it into ideal-sized groups your mind can handle, you are positioning yourself to accomplish your goals."

So when it comes to tackling that intimidating task that's been haunting you, break it down into sensible steps. Don't try and write a whole book in a month; write five hundred words a day until it's done.

TRICK YOUR BRAIN

The chance of succeeding is even higher if you block off time in your agenda for completing these smaller steps on the road toward achieving your "Big Task."

For example, if you want to tidy your attic, but you also know that you have to pick your child up from school at 3:00 p.m., there's not

 It's always better to make a start on your goals rather than never doing anything at all.

much point in telling yourself you will complete the job in one go. It's much more realistic to block out three hours of your time in the morning to get started, and then create another block later in the week in which you'll finish it. During those three hours, turn off all distractions: put your phone on silent and switch off your computer. Why? Because every time you do something else, it's estimated that your brain needs ten to twenty minutes to regain focus.

Another way to get things done when you're not in the right frame of mind is to commit just a tiny amount of time to your big job. This is a favorite method of Fokke Kooistra, a Dutch organizational coach. "What really helps me is to say to myself, 'I'm not in the mood for this and don't know if I'm going to be able to do it, but I will work on it for ten minutes. After that, if I still feel like it's not going to work, then I'll stop,'" Kooistra says. "Nine times out of ten, you become completely consumed by the task or you will have made so much progress that you think, 'I'm going to keep going.' You succeed in breaking through the resistance in your head by tricking yourself with the permission to stop after ten minutes without feeling guilty."

IT'S BETTER TO DO SOMETHING

Another thing Kooistra considers to be important is seeing the humor in the Importance Trap concept and the ways our brains work. Don't let the fact you haven't started a project yet intimidate you; it won't help and, in fact, it can make things worse. Not only will you feel even more

guilty about not achieving your goals, the tasks themselves will also start to feel too demanding. "Sometimes, I have to laugh at how I go about things," Kooistra admits. "I think, 'How funny, look at how evasive I'm being.' This is another key to making progress on your big goals: being able to put things in perspective. Life is not perfect, some projects will never be finished, and there are always tasks you'll find it hard to make time for. It's important to know that it's okay to not finish everything, and that it's always better to make a start on your goals rather than never doing anything at all. As Tracy puts it, "Do something. Do anything."

When it came to executing the renovation of my old, broken-down kitchen, it was my father who finally encouraged me to take action last year, after I had called him because my kitchen sink had flooded again. He asked a friend of his to come to my house, take some measurements, draw up some plans, and schedule the work. Not six months from now, but *now*. I panicked, but it turned out to be a good idea. Why? Because now, every time I make coffee or a sandwich, I get a tiny feeling of jubilation. Why hadn't I done this years ago?

WANT TO KNOW MORE?

- *Time Surfing: The Zen Approach to Keeping Time on Your Side* by Paul Loomans

- *Eat That Frog!: 21 Great Ways to Stop Procrastinating and Get More Done in Less Time* by Brian Tracy

MINDFUL DRAWING

BY CAROLINE BUIJS

*Mindful drawings don't have to be good;
they don't even have to be finished. More than anything,
mindful drawing is about simply doing it.*

W hether you have been wielding your pencil for years or just started drawing, mindful drawing might just help you see the world in richer detail. Noticing more (the literal meaning of mindfulness) is a skill that you can learn by meditating. By focusing your attention on your breathing during meditation, you become aware of your thoughts. But you can also practice noticing things in other ways—and drawing is one of them.

Mindful drawing is different from regular drawing, says British artist and creative mindfulness teacher Wendy Ann Greenhalgh. It is not complicated; you simply draw with more attention and awareness than you normally might.

SHARPEN THE POINTS

When you draw mindfully, you become more aware of all levels of detail: Colors become more intense; light and shadow become more distinct. The more you practice mindful drawing, the more you pay attention and see.

But what's the best way to begin? Organize your pencils on a cleared tabletop and sharpen the points to send the message to your mind that drawing is something special for you and that you are about to begin. Then, focus not only on your breathing, but also on three other things: the movement of your pencil on the paper; your eye-hand coordination (particularly when drawing an object), and the subject of your drawing. You are sometimes then able to pause your thoughts for a moment, giving you space to take in the world around you.

DOODLING

According to Greenhalgh, doodling is a great way to start. Doodling reconnects you to the physical aspect of drawing: You aren't drawing

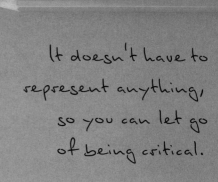

It doesn't have to represent anything, so you can let go of being critical.

anything specific, so you can focus wholly on your hands and the movements you are making.

A key element of mindfulness is a beginner's mind; this is what helps you focus on the act itself, and not on the success or failure of the outcome. You draw with no expectations but plenty of curiosity. Explore the colors of your new pencils, or chalk, or what it's like to use a toothbrush as a paintbrush. When you are drawing with a beginner's mind, you can experiment as you please.

Even collecting objects to draw can be an exercise in mindfulness. A tin can, a small toy, an oddly shaped branch, a discarded rubber band: Even things that are not "beautiful" can be interesting to draw.

EXERCISE 1: SELF-PORTRAIT

When we look in the mirror or see photos of ourselves, we may have a critical reaction. We might think our nose is too big, our eyes are too small, or our ears are crooked. However, when you look at your face with an artist's eye, features that are striking and unique about your face become interesting to draw. Remember: The portrait doesn't have to be an exact likeness; it's a drawing and not a photograph. If successful, it will capture something of your mood or

> "Nobody sees a flower—
> really—it is so small
> it takes time—we haven't
> time—and to see takes
> time, like to have a
> friend takes time."
>
> —Georgia O'Keeffe (1887-1986), American artist

personality. According to Greenhalgh, you can capture "not just what the eye can see, but also what the heart and mind can understand."

- Use a sheet of (at least) 11 x 17-inch paper. This will allow you to draw a life-size version of your face and head.

- Choose a mirror that easily shows your head and shoulders. Arrange it at an angle where you can draw comfortably.

- A soft pencil works best for this exercise.

- Give yourself different time lengths: Try drawing a portrait in two, five, ten, and twenty minutes, which can help distract you from focusing too much on the "perfect" result.

- View your face as if you are seeing it for the first time. This isn't easy, but worth a try.

- Look to find the lines and curves in your face, the light and shadow, and the texture and shape. Observe the color of your eyes, your hair, and your skin.

- Acknowledge the presence of any criticisms that may appear and then let them go again.

Try to simply experience your face as you see it in this moment.

EXERCISE 2: DRAW TO SEE

The act of seeing is a key aspect of all drawing. Greenhalgh recalls the first time she really saw a rose. "That summer day I thought I was pretty much 'done' with the rose," she writes. "I didn't think there was much more I could take in, but I carried on looking anyway. And as I did, everything seemed to shift. I suddenly noticed gradations in the shades of pink on the petals, which I leaned in closer to see better. I stopped looking and started really seeing."

- Draw with your favorite materials, but use just one color.

- Pick an inanimate object from nature: a flower, a stone, or a shell, for example.

- Take the time to really see the object. Use all your senses: hold it, touch it, smell it.

- Start drawing, and try not to look at the paper.

- Try drawing without lifting your pencil off the paper.

- Keep your hand loose and relaxed, and let it follow the movement of your eyes as they "trace" the lines of your object.

- Keep your attention on the object that you are drawing. Spend at least ten minutes drawing and redrawing it.

- Remember: This exercise is about seeing and experiencing, not about copying what you see.

- When you are done, take a moment to sit quietly and track your breathing.

According to Greenhalgh, "Most people find that . . . the lines are loose and expressive, and aspects of the object—its form or texture, for example—jump out in amazing detail and accuracy, even if the drawing as a whole doesn't look like the object it was inspired by."

EXERCISE 3: EXPLORE A LANDSCAPE

If you're someone who likes to be outdoors and spend time in nature, but not always wanting to go for a walk or run, try landscape drawing.

- Find a place outside that you love to look at and where you can sit comfortably.

- Look around with an open mind. Don't forget to also take in the sounds, the smells, and what you sense and feel: Pick a leaf and rub it between your fingers.

- By looking carefully and taking your time, you will gradually notice things: patterns in the bark of a tree, or the textures of the earth.

- Once you have identified what you want to draw, choose either the details or the big picture.

- If you start with the details, try making four different detail drawings on one sheet of paper. Each drawing is a meditation.

- If you prefer drawing the landscape as a whole, start by faintly sketching the relative positions of everything, starting in the middle of your page and working outwards.

- Done? Ask yourself if you now see or experience the landscape differently.

WANT TO READ MORE?

- *Mindfulness & the Art of Drawing: A Creative Path to Awareness* by Wendy Ann Greenhalgh

"I CAN'T DO IT"

We all hear that critical inner voice that pops up while we are drawing, saying, "This is worthless; throw it away." Here's how Wendy Ann Greenhalgh suggests you respond:

- Stop drawing and rest your hand on the paper. Focus on what the pencil feels like in your fingers, and on your breathing. This is the best way to deal with the thinking-mind, when it's gone into critical mode.

- Do acknowledge the voice, but don't dwell on the criticisms. Keep your attention focused on your hands and breath.

- If you keep getting drawn into critical thinking, bring your focus back to your body and breath, and use these as mindful anchors.

LIFE LESSONS LEARNED

===== BY CAROLINE BUIJS =====

It's common to wish we'd arrived at certain realizations about life earlier than we did. We asked four illustrators to tell us—in words and pictures—what life truths they wish they had understood sooner.

AGNES LOONSTRA
agnesloonstra.nl • @agnesloonstra

`"Everything will continue to go well as long as I say 'no' to something once in a while."`

"For a long time, I thought that my schedule always had to be full," Loonstra says. "It became a compulsion. Having a busy life felt like a reassurance, but in the long run, it had the opposite effect. I now know that it's not necessary to experience everything or to go to every event, and that skipping a party or even just doing nothing can also be heavenly. I can't be creative until I've struck a balance between receiving stimuli and processing them. Luckily, I've never suffered from a burnout, but I have been on the verge of one. I'm actually thankful for that experience because it was what helped me discover that everything will continue to go well as long as I say 'no' to something once in a while."

I'VE BEEN A VEGETARIAN SINCE CHRISTMAS 2018.

I WANTED TO BE ONE LONG BEFORE THAT, BUT IT SEEMED COMPLICATED, IN PRACTICAL TERMS.

WHEN I'M BUSY AND HAVE DEADLINES, IT'S SO MUCH EASIER TO JUST STICK TO A ROUTINE.

Grandma's (beef) goulash.

BUT WHAT ABOUT MY FAVORITE CHILDHOOD DISH?!

NOT EATING MEAT TURNS OUT TO BE EASIER AND TASTIER THAN I THOUGHT.

Krautsalat (without Speck)

Potato goulash!

+ I FOUND A TRADITIONAL VEGETARIAN VARIATION FROM THE SAME PERIOD AND REGION, WITH THE SAME FLAVORS. THIS BRINGS ME JUST AS CLOSE TO MY GRANDMA AS I WAS BACK THEN.

DEBORAH VAN DER SCHAAF

deborahvanderschaaf.nl
@deborahvanderschaaf

"Becoming a vegetarian really opened my eyes."

"I have really loved animals ever since I was a child and actually don't understand why it took so long for me to become a vegetarian," Van der Schaaf says. "I was in the supermarket around Christmastime, and all those special traditional meat packages suddenly became too much for me, from one minute to the next. Now I've got today's trends on my side, of course: I am really impressed by the people who were already vegetarians during a time when they would be mocked for eating tofu. I'm originally from South Tyrol, and although it's in Italy, many of the traditional dishes originate from Austrian cuisine. My grandmother made the best goulash for a table full of family members. A recipe for the variation using potatoes also turns out to be in her old cookbooks. This veggie goulash uses exactly the same stew sauce made with tomatoes, marjoram, and caraway seeds, but you add *gremolata* (a zesty Italian herb sauce) at the end. Becoming a vegetarian really opened my eyes, including taking a really close look at old habits: I apparently am more flexible and have more willpower than I thought. This might also apply to taking a long trip on my own, taking a class in something outside of my professional field, or maybe even moving to a house outside the city with some animals and plenty of greenery."

MARLOES DE VRIES

marloesdevries.com • @marloesdevee

"I'm just fine the way I am."

"I was drinking coffee in a café, watching people come in, and realized that there's a thin line between trying to satisfy other people's expectations of you and acting completely different," De Vries says. "'Acting completely different' is something an entire group then tries to do, creating yet another specific expectation you will want to meet. You never become yourself this way. It took me a long time to become myself, by the way. When I was a teenager, I desperately tried to fit in, which included dyeing my hair pink, but when I was around twenty-eight I really began to rebel against everything; mostly I didn't want to fit into the perfect picture. The things that made me different, such as my love of the Star Wars movies and LEGO, I really exaggerated, driven purely by my insecurity. I've mellowed out a lot since then. Whenever I'm feeling good about myself, I need other people's validation a lot less than I used to. Looking back, I wish I had had someone in my younger years who could have impressed upon me that I'm just fine the way I am. Staying true to who you are is actually what makes you unique."

YOU try SO HARD
TO BE different From
EVERY ONE ELSE
That YOU'RE STARTING
TO LOOK
Like every ONE
THAT TRIES
TO be
DIFFERENT.

WHICH IS
EVERY ONE.

MARLOES
DE VRIES

That I would meet amazing, weird, and extraordinary people, and that these people would become my friends

Sometimes you really should treat yourself to new shoes

JUST PEARFECT

Fresh flowers make me happy

Putting on fun clothes is another way of making a statement

What I wish I had known sooner...

Walking through the dunes can work wonders when I'm low on energy

NERDS are the best

VALESCA VAN WAVEREN
valescavanwaveren.com
@valescavanwaveren

`"Trying to conform to everyone`
`else is a hopeless task."`

"I'm somewhat of a nerd, a waverer, naive, and slightly slow,"
Van Waveren says. "I might also be a bit odd. These were the last
things I wanted to be when I was younger. I thought everything
would work out in the end for me and my relationships with other
people as long as I was just as brazen, funny, attractive, or popular
as they were. Because of course this is what we all ultimately
want: to feel a connection. But trying to conform to everyone
else is a hopeless task: In the end, who is everyone else? It's
something that's constantly changing. And suddenly becoming
brazen or attractive is something that only happens in those
coming-of-age movies. It's best to just want to be more like
yourself instead of hiding or being a chameleon. I wish I had found
out sooner that true, honest, and authentic friendships really do
exist . . . friendships—with colorful, kind, strong, amazing people
who help to remind me who I am—really do exist."

THE UNEXPECTED

Paths

ARE OFTEN THE

Most

Beautiful

- DAMIAAN DENYS

RETHINKING PROBLEMS AS OPPORTUNITIES

BY SJOUKJE VAN DE KOLK

We like to have everything under control, to strive for a perfect life. But in this interview with Damiaan Denys, philosopher and professor of psychiatry at the University of Amsterdam, we learn that imperfections and bad times may actually take us further in life.

▶ Has There Been an Increase in the Number of People with Psychological Problems?

Not necessarily. The taboo surrounding psychological problems has decreased, though, and we are more open to acknowledging them than before. Diagnostic methods have improved, and recognition of various disorders has increased, too, which can make it appear as if more people are suffering from them.

▶ Have Changes in Society in General Also Played a Role?

Absolutely, and in particular the way individualism has become the norm. Fewer people now identify with a group on the basis of a shared religion or ideology. It's every person for themself. The improvement of our living standards also plays a role. As paradoxical as it may sound, our general societal wealth is causing an increase in our psychological suffering. The moment our basic needs are being met—food and drink, a roof over our head, and a basic level of security—we start questioning other aspects of our life. Only then do we get around to pondering issues such as happiness, or the lack of it, and the meaning of life.

▶ So Things Are Going So Well That We Start Worrying About Ourselves?

In a sense, yes. But there is more to it, such as the fact that our living standards have increased so much that they no longer contribute to our quality of life. I think that the world we live in, here in the overwhelmingly privileged West at least, offers far too many choices. If you have the means, you can pick from among forty-two kinds of jam or five hundred different cars, and travel to thousands of different holiday destinations. You can choose among hundreds of different career options, decide to have children or not, and so forth. Of course, a small group of people are in a position to avail themselves of all the fantastic opportunities. But a larger group of people wrestle with all these options.

WRESTLING WITH YOUR TROUBLES MAKES YOU *more Creative*

▶ Where Does It All Lead?

People used to take life as it came. These days, we want to control everything all the time, but a couple hundred years ago, people had no idea whether it would rain on any given day. And if it did, they would find shelter under a tree, or pop into a café and have a drink. Now our weather apps tell us exactly when it's going to rain, but still we stress about getting caught in a storm. We've become so used to the predictive nature of our environment that we are knocked off balance very quickly when something doesn't go as planned. Advertising and media feed our fears: fear of being uninsured, of wearing the wrong brand of clothing, of not driving the safest car available. There is a lack of confidence in how things are, in how life unfolds.

▶ But People Are Responsible for Their Own Lives, Aren't They?

Yes, they are now, because of individualism. But it didn't used to be that way. In the past, religious communities were important, or your ideology. Individualism brought liberation, but also the need to do it alone. That includes having to give meaning to our life ourselves, and that's not always easy. So yes, life has become a heavier chore.

▶ We Have Such High Expectations . . .

That's right. We all want to lead a meaningful and happy life, which is quite a big ambition. And when people are asked what they would like to achieve, their answer is usually something unrealistic. We seem to have forgotten that suffering is a natural part of life. There's this big idea that everything should be possible. We have trouble accepting that sometimes bad things do happen.

▶ Would It Be Better to Look That Unfair Reality in the Face?

Of course a number of things *are* possible if we try hard enough, but not as many as most people think. We tend to have very negative attitudes to everything that doesn't fit with what we perceive as "a happy life." Any shortfall is immediately perceived as an enormous problem. And actually acknowledging limitations is fundamental to being human. Even good things depend on circumstances in which things do not go the way we want.

» How Can the Pitfalls Improve Our Lives?

By wrestling our way through the things that go wrong, we become stronger and we're forced to be more creative. As individuals we're just not capable of designing our own lives right down to the last detail. How could I, with my limited brain, possibly choose and develop the best life for me all on my own? When things go wrong, or differently than we want—as in times of divorce or illness—we're forced to lead our life differently than we planned. They may bring us to places we would not ordinarily have chosen to visit. In my life, the best and most creative solutions were found because of the problems I encountered, not because of my successes.

» Should We Be Looking At Our Problems in a Different Way?

Sometimes things happen that are truly terrible. But trouble also undeniably provides an opportunity for change. It is not in our nature to enact change on our own; we generally feel a lot of aversion to it. But what if we embraced it? Imagine you have been at the same job for ten years and then suddenly you're laid off. Yes, that's terrible. But it does force you to do something else, and after three years you might come around to thinking that losing that job was a good thing. Life is hard work; it involves suffering and failure and leads to the most beautiful moments of creation. Trials and tribulations help us lead a richer life, even if it's not always comfortable.

» How Would You Define a Good Life?

For me a good life means being able to express my true self, in relationship to others and to the world. It's about making something, thinking of something, or creating something that wasn't there before. For me, personally, that's the most satisfying thing there is. It can be an individual pursuit, like painting, or a group activity, like playing volleyball or doing community work. The most beautiful thing is bringing about change in the world, together. I don't mean we all have to aspire to be Nelson Mandela; it's the little things that matter. Tending a garden or chatting with your lonely neighbor also makes the world a better place.

» And Then It Becomes Possible for Us to Let Go of That Desire for Happiness?

Happiness comes when we feel like we have realized ourself as a person in the world. For example, by patching up a relationship, making a painting or reading a challenging book. These are very in-the-moment things, but my hope is that they will substitute for seeking happiness in possessions, in curious illusions, and in unrealistic expectations of life. Expressing our own potential in transaction with the world—that's what it is all about. And then our life won't always be comfortable, but it will be fulfiling.

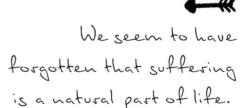

We seem to have forgotten that suffering is a natural part of life.

HOW DO YOU DEAL WITH THE UNEXPECTED?

▶ **Can you think of a situation or event in your life that happened unexpectedly?**

_____

_____

_____

▶ **How did this differ from what you had planned or pictured for yourself?**

_____

_____

_____

▶ **Did the new situation bring you to decisions and places you ordinarily wouldn't have chosen?**

_____

_____

_____

▶ **Looking back, can you name something good that came out of these circumstances?**

_____

_____

_____

EVERYTHING I CAN'T DO...

BY RIM VOORHAAR

We sometimes go to great lengths to try and bluff our way through life, pretending to be capable of anything and everything. But what if we allowed ourselves to make peace with all the things we can't do?

Recently, I found a cabinet on a sidewalk in my neighborhood and placed it right next to my front door, to serve as a community book exchange. Most of my neighbors were enthusiastic about my initiative; they said it was good for the community—particularly for a street whose high crime levels of a mere ten years ago had earned it a bad reputation. However, a spot of rain resulted in all the carefully collected books being collectively drenched. My cabinet lacked a decent roof—and doors.

My father—almost eighty years old now—can make anything with his hands. Give him a bunch of nails and three wooden boards and in four minutes he'll put together a new table for your kitchen that will last for a decade. Unfortunately, I do not have this skill. Whenever we have home improvement needs at our house, my wife is the one to pick up the hammer, drill, paintbrush, or saw. I, meanwhile, may hand her these tools, clean up afterward, and cook dinner, while playing with our five-year-old son. This division of labor catches me some flak, but I'm used to

it. What's more, I've started making a game of emphasizing all the things I'm not good at. And there are quite a few of them: I have no driver's license, for example. I don't do any sport seriously, but as a former sports reporter I do know a lot about the subject. The fact that I make dinner often sadly doesn't mean I can cook well. I'll never hear the end of how I once burned the pine nuts three times in a row. And did you know that iris bulbs look a lot like garlic?

Wife: "What did you do with the flower bulbs?"

Me: "What?"

Oh. Well, it tasted okay, the zucchini and iris bulb soup.

KEEPING UP APPEARANCES

All the things I'm no good at make for great stories to tell at parties—always good for a laugh. It's mostly in good fun, but I'm well aware there are enough people who also think I'm a bit of an idiot. And to be honest, I also used to feel like a bit of an idiot. I tried to become slightly handier around the house;

I have the how-to books to prove it. I thought if I just read a bit every night before falling asleep, I'd acquire some skills. And I did: I became really good at falling asleep very quickly. But despite all the books, our house's skirting boards are still loose. And unpainted. A few years ago, I gave in; I had to make peace with my lack of competence. It was a huge relief. Why do I have to be able to do all these things?

It's only human to have limitations. According to Dutch psychologist Ineke Lauwen, "People expect us to be able to do everything, or at least to pretend that we can. We have no choice but to live with our limitations. I think it's a mark of self-knowledge when someone admits they are not able to do something. When you do that, you are opening up the possibility to 'connect human-to-human in a real and authentic way.' And it often elicits a helpful response from the other person, too."

ACCEPTING THAT I KNOW NOTHING

Lauwen attended a series of lectures given by Dutch philosopher and musician Pablo Muruzábal Lamberti, about living like an

I may not be good at home improvement, but by simply admitting to it, other people are happy to pitch in. And this leads to a lot of friendships.

ancient stoic. She tells me that my story reminds her of Socrates. "Socrates would enter into dialogue with people from all layers of society, looking for someone wiser than he was," she says. "The Greek philosopher was doing this because the Oracle of Delphi had told him he was the wisest of all. By asking critical questions, he discovered that the people who claimed to know a lot really knew nothing. As everything that is human is unsure, Socrates then also claimed to know nothing. He was aware of his ignorance and humorously quipped, 'I know that I know nothing.'"

This particular insight was what made Socrates "knowledgeable again and therefore wise," and is also known as the Socratic paradox. Which, Lamberti says, connects with my sympathy for people who openly admit to not being good at something. "A person who claims to be able to do something but then turns out not to be able to do it obviously seems less trustworthy than a person who has enough self-knowledge to know what they are or aren't capable of doing," says Lamberti. "The same goes for wisdom. Saying you are wise does not show wisdom. The important thing is to apply yourself to seeking truth and develop . . . yourself. And, as Socrates would say: If you find truth, you have not searched hard enough yet."

For my little literary project, I didn't have to look far for a solution. The father of one of our kid's friends was so enthusiastic about the bookcase that he offered, out of the blue, to manufacture a couple of custom doors for it. Less than thirty minutes of work for him. It would have taken me. . . well, slightly longer, let's just leave it at that. For example, I'm guessing this guy didn't screw in all of the hinges of the cabinet doors upside down, like I did.

CHASING WHAT MATTERS

Why is it that, as men, we are expected to flex our muscles every so often? "It's because of the way we think in associative patterns," says Harold Bekkering, a Dutch professor of cognitive psychology. "In this particular case, the association is that you are a man, and a man should be able to do this and that. These stereotypes are deeply entrenched in our systems. Everyone creates their own model of the world, but that model is influenced by others and by what you see in commercials, books, films, and music. It's hard to accept that certain roles don't actually suit you in reality."

Bekkering has experienced the same as I have. "My wife is very handy and I'm not. She recently built a desk for our son, and she did it better than I would have." Nevertheless, these reverse male-female role models are not often fully accepted. Bekkering has a neighbor who frequently drops by when he needs help. "The other day, it was something to do with the fence in his yard," Bekkering says. "The neighbor asked, 'Harold, can you come and give us a hand?' I said I'd be happy to help lift stuff, but my wife would do a better job of actually putting it together. 'But you're the guy,' my neighbor said. 'Shouldn't you be doing these chores?'"

Bekkering says stereotypes are evolving. "Very slowly, appreciation is growing for men who also take care of their children, for example. But it's slow going, make no mistake. We only have ourselves to blame, and the stubbornness of our thinking patterns. For example, I love to play squash. I really enjoy it, and have accepted that I am not a great athlete; I just do sports to be physically active. But, the sports world is linked to a competitive thinking pattern: Sometimes after I lose a match I have trouble saying, 'Oh it doesn't matter, I enjoyed playing.' And what about when our kids play a soccer match? We ask them if they scored a goal. No one asks, 'Were you good at defense today?' So our kids learn that that's what matters."

WHAT *REALLY* MATTERS

The same happens in education. "Everything is expressed in points," Bekkering says. "If you do a good job, you get higher points. Whether you actually learned anything or not is of less importance. Our son is in primary school. He is learning about concepts such as the tropical rain forest. He is taught the right words to describe this forest, like hot (tropical), trees (forest), and precipitation (rain). But his actual thoughts about the rain forest ('I see Tarzan swinging his way through the trees on a vine') are not welcome."

Stereotypes again, says Bekkering. "We are forced to describe the world in the terms we once agreed upon as a group. The world is broken down into definitions and we all learn them by rote. But we are all living in our own individual model of the world. Each person experiences the world in their own unique way. Home improvement? Might not really be your thing. Maybe you want to make things with letters, maybe you want to write stories. That's building, too, isn't it?"

In the end, even I managed to succeed in hanging the doors on the bookcase. They even look fun, decorated with a drawing that can be colored in by the children in the neighborhood. Koosje Koene, an illustrator who lives on our street, volunteered to do it. As a thank you, I offered her an old-fashioned cup of coffee and a slice of cake. I may not be good at home improvement, but by simply admitting to it, other people are happy to pitch in. And this leads to a lot of friendships.

FAREWELL TO WHO WE THOUGHT WE WERE

BY PEGGY VAN DER LEE

Maybe you thought you'd be a trendsetter, a world traveler, an inspiring speaker. But then you're not. And maybe it doesn't matter; maybe this realization can be the start of something new.

Saying goodbye to the things we thought or hoped to be is something that we all contend with, according to psychotherapist Riekje Boswijk. Maybe you thought you'd be an extrovert, making friends with all sorts of strangers at a party, but then you discover you'd rather head straight to the people you know. Or you thought you were a real team player, but slowly you realize you like doing things yourself. Also common: You hoped to be flexible, but on closer inspection it turns out you don't respond well to change.

At some point, you develop "lots of ideas about what you want and what you could be," Boswijk says. Then, "about halfway through life it's natural to take stock. What does my life look like? What suits me and what doesn't? You may find the things you expected of yourself are not necessarily the ones that suit you."

THE PLAN VS. THE REALITY

According to Boswijk, the mismatch between who we are and what we want to be is largely the result of the idealized images in our head, driven by external pressures. And that pressure seems to be increasing. "All those perfect lives in TV series, magazines, and on social media make you feel that you're only a success if you've seen the whole world, have a cheerful, attractive family, and your home has the latest colors on the walls," she says. "Besides that, you must have certain qualities: It seems that everyone must be an extrovert. You must find It easy to tell your story, start a conversation, share your life on social media, and present yourself in a minute. But the reality is that half of humanity is not outgoing at all. If you have to pretend to be an extrovert when really you're not, then actually you're rejecting yourself, whereas being an introvert is a wonderful trait."

AUTHENTICITY AND WELL-BEING

Psychologist Abigail Mengers conducted a study at the University of Pennsylvania about the relationship between being yourself and

*To feel if something suits you, you sometimes have to let go of an old idea about yourself.*

your well-being. Mengers reports that it's not only unpleasant, but actually unhealthy to expect something from yourself that is not in you at all. Like starting a mindless conversation at the coffee machine when you really can't stand idle chitchat. As humans, we have a natural need to belong to a group. That's why we cross our own boundaries at times just to avoid being alone. Mengers's research shows that people need to be authentic. According to her research, "participants with greater conscious awareness of their true states, emotions, and thoughts reported feeling more satisfied with their lives. This demonstrates a strong relationship between authenticity and well-being."

It can be a huge relief to accept that you are not what you thought. To stop and reveal your real self. When Boswijk was writing loads of books about grief, saying goodbye, anger, and consolation, she was invited to speak on the subjects on TV. "Not such a bad idea," she says, "because, of course, doing that helps sell books and I thought my subject was important." But it was quickly apparent to her that she couldn't respond as freely on TV as she needed to. "I don't talk in one-liners. It wasn't working. It gave me the justification to say it didn't suit me."

HOW DO YOU KNOW WHO YOU ARE?
Accepting who I am feels like it should bring a sense of relief, but I don't always feel that peace in myself. Because I believe in something else: that who I am and what suits me might not be set in stone. That every phase is different, and that I can change.

I sometimes wonder if I shouldn't accept the fact that I'm a generalist. I'm a psychologist and journalist, and I've grown to know a lot about many psychological topics through all the stories I've written and the people I've interviewed. But I'm not a specialist in any one thing, like a heart surgeon who knows all about a vital organ and can save lives at crucial moments. Is that bad? I love doing and delving into everything. But I also would find it fascinating to have deep knowledge of one significant topic. It hasn't happened yet, but why couldn't that be different in another phase? Maybe it's who I am, too. Can you ever know who you really are?

PEOPLE CHANGE
You can't, says British philosopher Julian Baggini in his TED Talk, "Is There A Real You?" In fact, there is no such thing as an established self. There is only, says Baggini, a mountain of beliefs, desires, experiences, and sensations. Things you think and feel, depending on the people you meet, and the things you experience.

So we're not really "permanent" beings that undergo experiences; what we experience determines who we are. Baggini uses a waterfall as a metaphor: "Of course the water that flows through the waterfall is different every single instance. But it doesn't mean that the falls are an illusion. It doesn't mean it's not real. What it means is we have to understand what it is as something which has a history, has certain things that keep it together, but it's a process, it's fluid, it's forever changing."

Your real self is not something you find by looking deep enough inside; you create yourself. Which, Baggini believes, is liberating. "Because if you think that you have this fixed, permanent essence, which is always the same, throughout your life, no matter what, in a sense you're kind of trapped," he says. It adds something nice, in any case, for types like me who are looking for peace, but who also like keeping all options open.

"[Of course,] you need a little cooperation from life," says Boswijk. "I always tell my children that life is a train, it just trundles by. Opportunity awaits in every carriage and if one appeals to you, jump on it! To feel if something suits you, sometimes you have to let go of an old idea about yourself."

Not that a huge introvert will suddenly turn into a huge extrovert. Baggini and Boswijk agree on that. "But as an introvert," says Boswijk, "you may prove to be an inspiring speaker if you can talk about topics that are really dear to you." What's important, she says, is to stay feeling good: Am I doing this because I like exploring new options, because I want to do it? Or am I doing it because I feel I must, because everyone else is doing it? If you set the compass correctly, there's nothing wrong with trying a new direction now and then. Or trying again. Or watching that passing train and deciding which wagon to jump on . . .

How to Fail

BY LIDDIE AUSTIN

Failing isn't good or bad or even particularly useful:
It's simply a part of life. Let's explore the healthiest approaches
to dealing with the pain that inevitably comes with it.

"Try talking to the person sitting next to you about a time you failed." I'm listening to a presentation given by British futurist and writer James Wallman, who achieved fame with his book *Stuffocation*. The topic of his latest book, *Time and How to Spend It*, is finding out what makes us happy. Wallman has just argued how liberating it is to remove "the veil of perfection." After all, yes, life is wonderful, but it can also be a pretty big struggle sometimes. According to psychological research, people who can talk about their failures are happier than people who always just keep up appearances. Everyone can relate to stories of failure, and this evokes empathy. And Wallman clarifies this when he shares that "empathy is connection, connection is relationships, relationships are the key to happiness."

In other words, bring on the stories of failure. I feel a slight sense of panic coming on. Am I supposed to tell a complete stranger that I had no clue my ex-boyfriend was unhappy and was seeing someone else for a really long time before he left me, an event that felt to me like it happened overnight? That I am a complete failure as a driver? That I recently took my cat to the vet far too late, and that he probably couldn't get better because of my mistake?

Fortunately, a woman sitting next to me jumps at the opportunity to share her failures. She tells a story about when she first wore high heels as a teenager and how one of the heels broke as she was on her way to a night out on the town. She stood at the bus stop, a shoe on one foot and nothing but pantyhose on the other. I breathe a sigh of relief and talk about how I once went for an important job interview wearing a borrowed dress that I thought was very conservative, but (as I was later enlightened) actually had a very plunging neckline. I was totally oblivious to this detail at the time, but the person who interviewed me continued to remind me of this long afterward. Because yes, in spite of the dress, I got the job.

The moments of failure that are shared after that don't really seem that awful. Most of them are funny and not so painful. As helpful as it apparently can be to share these stories of failure, though, this is clearly something that isn't that easy for any of us.

FAILURE IS THE NEW SUCCESS

After the self-help industry applauded success for so many years, failure is now demanding its place in the spotlight. Books, articles, and inspirational talks on disappointment seem to be everywhere. Perfection is out—failure is the new success. British author Elizabeth Day started a podcast on failure based on the idea that she grew more from the things that went wrong than the things that seemed to go well. She interviews famous people about their three biggest failures. Ironically enough, the podcast is a huge success, and Day has also authored a book based on it. Journalist and author Marianne Power describes in her book *Help Me!* how she spent a year living her life according to the lessons prescribed in several popular self-help books. Her conclusion is that it was a wasted effort. "I don't have to better myself; I'm fine the way I am, flaws and all," she tells me.

Why have imperfection and failure suddenly become so popular? Friend and foe generally agree that it has to do with how important personal success has become in our society. We are expected to succeed in everything we do, preferably in full view for everyone to see on social media. In a climate like this, a mistake is quickly viewed as a disaster, it's up to you to shape your life, and if you can't do this, it's your own fault. No wonder so many people feel like a failure these days.

In response to all the pressure, we really want—we *need*—to hear that failure is a part of life. And justifiably so, because every process is characterized by elements that inevitably go wrong. Without failure, we can't learn or discover anything new. There's no success without it.

LEARNING FROM LIFE

But success is what we weren't supposed to talk about, right? What's striking about this scenario is that ultimately, via a shortcut, you still end up at success anyway. Mistakes are seen as opportunities to learn from that can make you even more successful. "It's the Steve Jobs version of failure," says Dutch writer Marian Donner. "Initially, Apple went broke a few times, and each time, Jobs came back stronger and ultimately became a huge success. This isn't very helpful [because] by only seeing failure as something you're supposed to learn from, you make it harder on yourself. You're supposed to take advantage of the good, and the bad. This is no easy task."

Saakje Bakker, a Dutch expert in the field of failure also points out that failure is often associated with achievement. "It's more like, 'Watch how successfully I'm failing,'" she says. "Don't get me wrong, I do love success, but how great would it be to be able to let go of the pressure and try something that might also fail without having serious consequences?"

Failing isn't good or bad or particularly useful, but it can be very painful at times. Is there a healthy way of coping with it without having to turn it into something productive? Definitely, says Bakker. "One thing that really helps me is to see myself as an intern in life," she says. "It's

okay to learn things and not to have to do everything at once, or be the best at everything. I allow myself to try things—sometimes I succeed, which is great, but if I don't, it's not the end of the world. When you have an uninhibited outlook on life, curiosity often wins out over fear of failure when it comes to trying things."

Bakker recommends you go easy on yourself. "How do you talk to yourself when you do something wrong?" she asks. "Are you quick to be very critical and hard on yourself? The more lenient you can be with yourself, the better you'll be able to cope with mistakes. Try to see it this way: It didn't work out this time; better luck next time." What if you don't get a second chance? "It goes without saying that certain mistakes have huge consequences," she acknowledges. "In that case, you would have to accept full responsibility, including with respect to those you may have hurt. It may sound simple, yet it appears to be everything but this in practice. You feel guilty and ashamed and in my experience, there's a lot we're willing to do to not have to feel these emotions. This is why we tend to place the blame elsewhere for very big mistakes and play the victim. Getting comfortable with the uncomfortable: this is what we have to learn to be able to fail 'properly.' It's only by acknowledging our mistakes and seeing what we can do about it that we can eventually move on."

WE'RE ALL ALRIGHT

In her anti-self-help pamphlet (or "self-destruction guide"), Donner says that the frequent feeling of failure in today's world isn't an individual problem, but is caused instead by a society that is demanding the impossible of us to an increasing degree. Her advice is not to fall for it: "Don't optimize yourself," she says. "Waste time, just be yourself, instead of the

The more lenient you can be with yourself, the better you'll be able to cope with mistakes.

best version of yourself. Failure is the essence of being human; it just happens. You get old, love fades. And then you also die, which is the ultimate failure. By acknowledging that you're 'fallible,' you first undermine the system that dictates that you always have to be successful and happy. Mostly, you'll just discover that there can be a lot of beauty in failure. When I was young, I had big dreams of success, just like all the people I hung around with at the time. Very few of these came true for any of us. Life became a bit more trite than it had been in our fantasies: We had children, got normal jobs, and muddled through. Ultimately, we're all the same; that's the beauty of failure. Success is about setting yourself apart, being better than other people, rising above the rest. But life is fantastic enough as it is. By acknowledging that we're all creatures who fail and have dreams that get crushed by reality, you feel more connected to one another."

So Wallman is right: We don't have to act all secretive about the mistakes we make, if they're even really mistakes. Once you share them, some of them even appear to be very human, and others can be turned around and viewed as teachable moments. And yes, some mistakes are impossible to rectify. You'll have to live with them, as awful as it is. You're not perfect; shit happens, as they say. Eventually, you get back up and move on. For me, my cat's death, whether I was the cause of it or not, remains a sore spot for me. I hope to be able to turn this into something positive; I will undoubtedly be more attentive with my new kitten.

WANT TO KNOW MORE?

- *Time and How to Spend It: The 7 Rules for Richer, Happier Days* by James Wallman

- *How to Fail: Everything I've Ever Learned from Things Going Wrong* by Elizabeth Day.

- *Help Me!: One Woman's Quest to Find Out If Self-Help Really Can Change Her Life* by Marianne Power

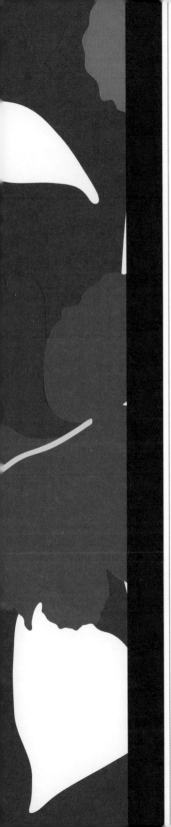
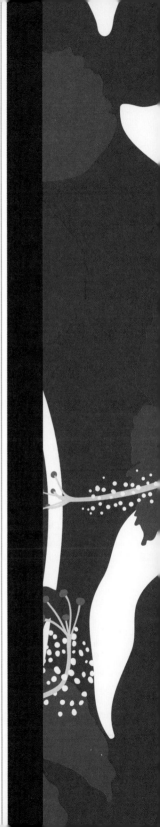

Chapter 5

LOVE YOUR IDLE TIME

IT MUST BE SOME KIND OF ILLNESS: There we are, finally listening to that podcast that's been on our list for months when, right in the middle of listening to it, we think, *Hmm, maybe we'd rather finish reading that book now.* And when we're reading the book, we suddenly remember we've got some laundry to do. And while we're folding laundry, we think, *Laundry, in this nice weather? Shouldn't we go somewhere—maybe to the beach?*

Because most of us have really packed schedules much of the time, it feels increasingly difficult to think of what we should do in the few empty hours we occasionally have. And on top of that, we also tend to be extremely practical and encumbered by a nagging sense of guilt. Just lounging on the couch may be fine for our teenagers, but we don't dare allow ourselves that luxury. Everything has to have a purpose (and, whenever possible, also earn us a pat on the back).

But doing nothing useful is actually *useful.* If we don't plan our days full of practical activities from minute to minute, we find there is room for wonder and surprise, to give our brains a break. And that break is very much needed. Collecting shells on the beach or arranging our books by color in the bookcase . . . what we may perceive as wasting time isn't a waste of time at all. It's just that we all need to commit to giving it some more practice.

HOW GOOD ARE WE AT NIKSEN?

BY ANNEMIEK LECLAIRE

The Dutch concept of niksen—*actively doing nothing—has gained popularity beyond the Netherlands. But what is it exactly, and how can we achieve it?*

A couple of times each day, I sit down in a chair overlooking the square in front of my house and open my windows. The storm in my head clears, and I take some distance from what I was doing so intensely just before. Is that what is meant by *niksen*? Or is a free afternoon without plans *niksen*? Or is it loafing around the house, doing some laundry, leafing through the newspaper?

BRAIN BREAK

At some point, the Dutch word *niksen* became a lifestyle trend. Articles about "the Dutch art of doing nothing" have appeared in international media for years. Various non-Dutch journalists picked up on this word in separate synchronicity and thought, *That's just what we need in these times of stress and burnout.* They may allude to the Netherlands' generous vacation leave (the Dutch have more days off per year than other Western countries) or the relative ease of working part-time in the country.

Olga Mecking, a Polish journalist who now lives in The Hague in the Netherlands, reported on *niksen* in the *New York Times*. "*Niksen*," she says, "is a Dutch word, but it's not a specifically Dutch cultural phenomenon." And surely, I ask her, it used to even have negative connotations?

Yes, says Mecking, "Participation and contribution has always been important in Dutch society—participating in the sense of contributing. Helping one another, paying visits to each other, learning the Dutch language if you're not from here, helping at school or other volunteer work. *Niksen* isn't really part of that culture of participation." According to Mecking, the fact that Dutch people have so many days off, or work part-time, doesn't mean that they're better at doing nothing, but that they theoretically have more room for it in comparison with, for example, workers in the United States, where being present at your work is so important. It also isn't true that Dutch people have fewer obligations: "The Dutch have an agenda as full as anyone else," Mecking says. "There are just other things in it."

Still, there's nothing to stop the Dutch or anyone from making a habit out of *niksen* now, because it's important to stop what you are

Take a break that spares your brain and eyes: fiddling, loafing, lazing, lolling, idling, messing around.

doing at various moments, even if only to give your brain a break. Mecking agrees. "I see *niksen* as a form of self-care that is easier to put into practice than other kinds of relaxation," she says. "As a way to take care of yourself, it is a lot easier than, for example, the Danish *hygge* or Japanese tidying á la Marie Kondo. For *hygge* you have to go get candles, pillows, and food, and with the Kondo technique you have to declutter your house. That's a lot of work—and self-care immediately becomes work again. For *niksen* you don't have to do anything."

OLD RUST BIN

Niksen makes you more creative and productive, and prevents you from breaking down. "We maintain focus by using our attention network," says Dutch brain researcher and author Niki Korteweg. "Concentrated thinking takes effort," she says. "You can tell because your thoughts stray; the head can only maintain such keen focus for a limited time. When you defocus, a different area in your brain is activated: the default network. This is the state of rest of the brain in which thoughts can stray. We start to muse and daydream; we can imagine things." That is why, according to Korteweg, defocusing is important for our associative capacity and our creativity. "The same default network is also active in people who are in a creative flow: for example, jazz musicians during improvisation," she says. "Being able to switch easily between being focused and not at all is an important skill for creativity."

A little *niksen* also ensures that you get more done afterward. Diverting your attention completely away from something refreshes your mind. American research shows that short breaks reinforce concentration. What's more, those pauses are necessary to prevent you from burning out. Korteweg herself writes in her book that she put her brain through years of "marinating it in stress hormones, turning it from a flexible thinking machine into an old rust bin—rickety, slow, and unreliable. As if someone had thrown a shovel of sand into the gears." Meditation, sports, and sleeping helped her to get back on top. "You can work seriously hard if you just take serious breaks, too," she writes.

HOW TO RECOGNIZE A CROWDED BRAIN

If you're feeling low-energy, aren't getting anything done, aren't achieving your goals, have no more creative ideas, are repeating mistakes, and feeling easily overwhelmed: These are all signs of a crowded brain. Take them seriously and make timely adjustments before you can no longer do anything at all, warns psychiatrist and brain researcher Srini Pillay, author of *Tinker Dabble Doodle Try*. Pillay calls defocusing "an intelligent form of letting go."

That is why stress scientists nowadays insist on the need to take breaks. Not just pausing, but a break that spares your brain and eyes: fiddling, loafing, lazing, lolling, idling, messing around. That could be doing the laundry, taking a shower, going for a walk. *Niksen* doesn't mean sitting motionless in a chair, but should entail activities that you can walk away from just like that, writes Canadian author Rachel Jonat in her book *The Joy of Doing Nothing*. Your brain doesn't need to do anything; you feel peaceful and relaxed. So watching an action movie is not *niksen*. Neither is checking Instagram. "News and opinions also cause persistent stress in the brain cells," says Korteweg.

SLEEP BETTER

Toward the end of the summer, a circus always comes to my city, and I see the lines of flickering lights hanging over the pink-and-white striped circus tent, between the tall, green trees. As winter rolls in, the owner of the local organic store starts selling fresh donuts in front of his door from a stall exactly under my window. I only started to learn how to properly engage in *niksen* during a year in which I decided to slow down a bit. I had had enough of the daily rat race and decided to live a little more and do a little less. What I noticed was that by doing nothing, daily points of attention made room for deeper thoughts and feelings. Only as soon as I stopped what I was doing did I notice that I was irritated, sad, worried, or rushed.

The fact that I now recognize those feelings in my *niksen* during the day may be one of the reasons why I sleep better these days. Previously, my uneasiness only surfaced in the middle of the night. My brain suddenly went on

PRACTICE *NIKSEN* OVER PROCRASTINATION

You know that moment when you desperately need to start something, but keep postponing it? Canadian author Rachel Jonat advises turning that into a *niksen* moment. Get away from your computer if you don't feel like getting started. Wander around, look outside, make a cup of tea, go for a walk. . . . Chances are that you can start fresh again afterward.

alert, like a radar that detects an incoming enemy and sounds an alarm. I could pretty much forget about getting any more sleep. Now I make time for those concerns during the day, and they no longer pounce on me at night.

A SWEET LITTLE LUXURY

Niksen used to effortlessly be part of our lives—it was an unsought gift. Riding the bus, standing in line, driving to our vacation destination: There were no distractions. What else could you do? Stare into thin air, whittle a piece of wood with your pocketknife, have a chat. Nowadays, taking a rest has become a skill. We have to learn how to do it again, amid the constant bombardment of apps, text messages, and so on. Taking a break can be tricky if you're used to being "on," regardless of your degree of concentration, says Jonat. Our brains need to learn new habits. Take the time, she advises. Sit it out. Life becomes harder, the busier and more stressful it is.

Scaling back is also difficult in some periods of your life where there is simply a lot of stuff that has to be done. If your life offers little room for breaks, start at the edges of the day, Jonat advises. Ten minutes before you get up or fifteen minutes before you go to sleep. Just do nothing for a bit before you put your feet on the cold floor tiles or turn off the light. Do it when you have to wait for something, or after work, or before you pick up the kids. Do it just after eating dinner, before cleaning the kitchen. You can even make it into a family ritual by instituting a group "*niksen* moment." Jonat calls that time for ourselves "a sweet little luxury." And once you have practiced for a while, *niksen* could start lasting longer. According to Jonat, the fringe hours are very suitable, for example after dinner when the table is cleared. With the telephone on night mode and the TV off, two hours of relaxation are yours.

For myself, it sometimes leads to me tearing out pretty pictures from magazines, listening to new music, rearranging the bulletin board, browsing through a cookbook, or baking something. Doing nothing is a necessary run-up to doing something that I actually really enjoy.

If your life offers little room for breaks, start at the edges of the day: ten minutes before you get up or fifteen minutes before you go to sleep.

ALL OVER THE PLACE

To really take your distance, you need longer periods of nothing. A weekend or a week. If you're lucky, even longer. I have the luxury that I can do that regularly on an island where my parents have a house. When I'm there, I go for walks, sit on the deck looking at the wood pigeon flutter its wings, lie in the garden staring at the sky, and hum while I hang the laundry on the line—my thoughts everywhere and nowhere at the same time. Only during those less busy days do I get around to addressing the bigger questions: Am I doing okay? Am I doing something suitable for me? Am I seeing the people I want to see? And if that period lasts long enough, the questions eventually fall away and I'm just moving with the rhythm of the day, with the season.

So try to go into nature more often, hang your laundry up with wooden clothespins, rake the leaves, sniff the scent of freshly baked goods: This way you, too, can incorporate *niksen* into your life.

WANT TO READ MORE?

- *Niksen: Embracing the Dutch Art of Doing Nothing* by Olga Mecking

- *The Joy of Doing Nothing: A Real-Life Guide to Stepping Back, Slowing Down, and Creating a Simpler, Joy-Filled Life* by Rachel Jonat

- *Tinker Dabble Doodle Try: Unlock the Power of the Unfocused Mind* by Srini Pillay

- *Bored and Brilliant: How Spacing Out Can Unlock Your Most Productive and Creative Self* by Manoush Zomorodi

Calm-Down Posters

Sometimes a few well-chosen words
(and images) can be reassuring
when the world feels restless.
Choose between serene photographic
landscapes or illustrated feline comfort.

THE IDEAL OF CALM
EXISTS IN A SITTING CAT

YOU LEARN
SO MUCH
WHEN YOU
SIT STILL
AND LISTEN.

–Sylvia Plath

RELAX

GETTING
LOST IS
NOT A
WASTE
OF TIME.

–Jack Johnson

TIME SPENT
WITH CATS
IS NEVER WASTED

JUST SLOW
THINGS
DOWN AND
IT BECOMES
MORE
BEAUTIFUL.

–David Lynch

And now I remember
why nothing beautiful
happens quickly.

Growing always
takes time.

Like seasons.
Like change.

—@wilderpoetry

Waiting A BIT can Be very EFFECTive
-HOLM FRIEBE

PLEA FOR PASSIVITY

══ BY CATELIJNE ELZES ══

*Don't do it right away, just wait and see what happens.
In an interview, German economist, strategist, and author Holm Friebe
calls this the "stone strategy" and explains why it works so well.*

➤ Why Is the Stone Strategy So Important Now?

Our society emphatically values action. The world belongs to the ones who act; if you don't try, you'll never win, and so on. It's all about movement, change, innovation. But that's not always the best way. It often leads to wrong decisions in business, science, and politics. The tricky thing is that if we have the capability to take action, we often also feel the impulse to do it. But that impulse is based on emotion, especially in unclear situations where we can't see all the factors involved. Waiting, then, becomes a better strategy. A good example is if you get lost—outdoors in the real world, I mean, with a smartphone that's run out of battery and no GPS. If we assume that it's likely that people will eventually search for you, "staying put" is actually the best thing to do. Stay where you are, save your strength, and be economical with any supplies you have.

➤ How Can You Keep Still When Everything Is Moving So Fast?

It involves a shift in perspective. I don't know if it's true that things are moving "so fast." If you look at it another way, perhaps our pace of renewal has actually slowed down. When the BBC asked its listeners in 2005 what the best invention of all time was, the bike got almost 60 percent of the votes, and the Internet only 4 percent. The invention of the toilet lastingly improved the lives of billions of people. At the end of the nineteenth and beginning of the twentieth centuries, antibiotics, airplanes, cars, the radio, and the telephone were all invented. Those were big changes. What I want to say is that we should have more eye for continuity. Many fundamental things that exist now will still be around in fifty years. Distrust the mandate of change; you don't necessarily have to jump into line with *every* new trend. If your current habits are healthy and work for you, just keep on doing the things you already do.

Why Is It So Difficult?

Because it's not in our nature. Reacting quickly was important in the distant past to survive—fight or flight: thinking twice about it could be deadly. What also makes it difficult is that waiting is usually not appreciated. If your boss asks why sales figures are down and what is going to be done about it, answering that you don't know yet how things will develop, so it's better not to do anything won't make your boss happy. Passivity is seen as something negative, as if it is wasting time. But sometimes the right time to take action hasn't arrived yet, and you need to gather more information first, or wait for circumstances to change. The problem is that we often don't dare. We're afraid that others will get ahead of us, and take off with the prize. The Red Queen from the book *Through the Looking-Glass* says it so beautifully: "Now, here, you see, it takes all the running you can do, to keep in the same place. If you want to get somewhere else, you must run at least twice as fast as that!" In other words, standing still is falling behind. But you will never finish anything properly if you keep running. Because before you're done, you have to run after something new. People who achieve great things occasionally distance themselves and watch what happens. Take Steve Jobs. When he returned to Apple—then a small company—in 1998, he was asked what he was going to do. "I'm going to wait for the next big thing," Jobs replied. That turned out to be very clever in hindsight.

What's the Difference Between Your Strategy and Doing Nothing?

There are countless books about becoming calm inside, going back into nature, finding your inner self. As far as I am concerned, these only highlight the flipside of overstraining or burning out. I am proposing a strategy that you can apply in your work—for example, when you as a team want to make a decision about how to continue with a project—but also in your private life. It is not "doing nothing"; it is simply "not acting immediately." Doing less, actually doing almost nothing at all, but doing that bit of what you do with decisive effectiveness.

You Call It "Active Waiting," But What Does That Mean?

Don't numb yourself by zoning out on TV or the like. It can be valuable to do that occasionally, but it renders your brain activity very low. The best approach is to keep your senses sharp while you "wait." Make sure you can hear the grass grow. Stay outwardly tuned in while not focusing too much on your problem or its possible solution. Just like when foraging for mushrooms: If you only look at the ground very close to you, you won't find them. You have to wander around a bit, with your eyes everywhere, and then they find you. That may sound vague, but it's how it works. Be inviting and open. You don't discover new possibilities by searching for them very hard.

Sometimes the right time to take action hasn't arrived yet.

YOU will NEVER Finish ANYTHING PROPerLY IF you KEEP running

⟩ What If You Don't Know What You Want in Your Life?

My advice is to look at your life up until now. You will probably find many ingredients that can show you the way. Do what stones do: They move a bit, but they do not reinvent themselves every day, changing into a fish, flower, or butterfly. People are more like stones than we think. We are subject to gravity, and change slowly. It is easier to move with gravity. Roll down the hill instead of trying to push yourself up the hill. I am not a good self-help advisor. I don't want to make promises I can't deliver on. If you read my book, your life will not be changed. But maybe that's not a bad thing.

⟩ Can You Apply the Stone Strategy in Relationships?

For short-term effect, you can use the stone strategy rather well. Don't take too much action, don't respond too quickly to messages, don't run after someone. "Playing hard to get" may make you desirable, but in a long relationship it doesn't work well. Not responding and being unapproachable just creates more distance. Still, the stone strategy can yield some results in smaller ways, to take the rough edges out of quarrels for example. Let things rest, wait until they fade away, or, instead of fighting out a conflict to the end, put it on the shelf for a while. In emotional situations, we often tend to have overheated reactions; one word leads to another and so it escalates. Retreating early and allowing some time to pass is often the best thing you can do.

⟩ How Can We Use the Stone Strategy to Best Navigate the World of Social Media?

The most obvious advice would be to let it go, don't participate, retreat into your cocoon—but I'm not a fan of that. Social media can be positive. I think the most important thing is not to go along with the hysteria. Don't believe that a social medium is the next big thing that will bring us everything we don't have yet. Just keep thinking for yourself, don't expect too much, take some distance, and see if you can do something with it.

Slow-Down Puzzle Stickers

Here's how to create a bit of quiet
in your mind: Match the number on the
sticker with the number on the next page
and stick it in the correct space.
Slowly but surely, the image will emerge.

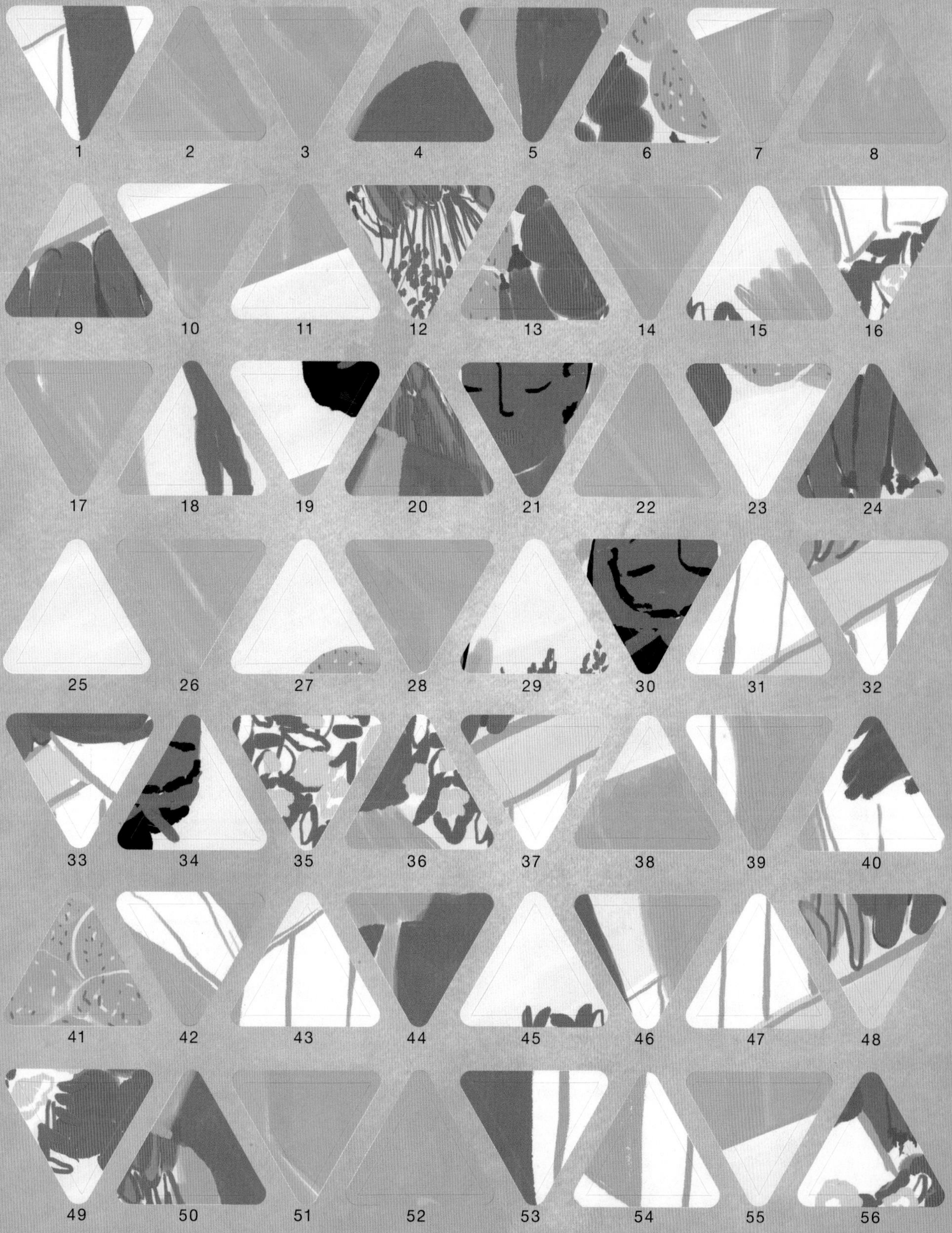

ILLUSTRATION **KAREN SCHIPPER**

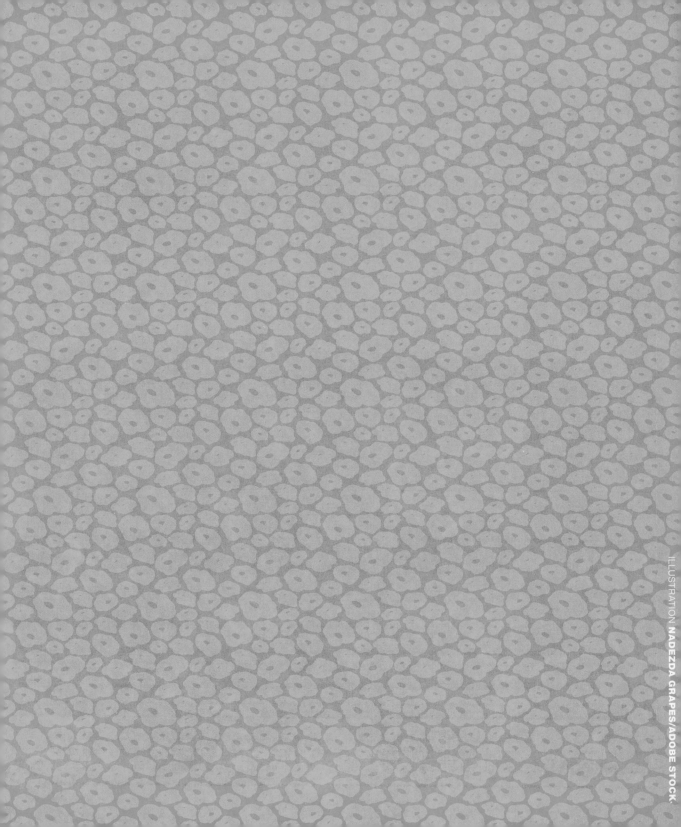

The tiny Pleasures in my Garden
by Hadas Hayun

Moths and butterflies aren't just beautiful, but also invaluable to the garden.

Feeling the sun, smelling the soil after it has rained, seeing the plants change and grow: Working in the garden stimulates all the senses.

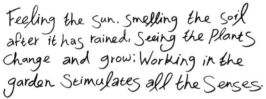

There's nothing better than growing your own food...

I love upcycling and can turn anything into a plant pot.

The birds love visiting the birdhouse.

....and snacking on the strawberries that you have planted.

Too Little Time?

== BY MARISKA JANSEN ==

How often do we feel like we don't have enough time?
Even though our schedules are full and our to-do lists are long,
the number of hours in the day remains the same. How do our perceptions
of time work, but mostly how can we manage to feel less rushed?

I recently realized I constantly have the feeling that I never have enough time—in the mornings, when I'm rushing to get the kids to school before getting to an appointment, or later, as I'm sitting at my computer, the hours flying by. When I look at everything on my to-do list, I think a day should actually have thirty hours. But the real problem isn't the limited number of hours; it's the fact that I cram as many activities as I can into each day, and underestimate how much time each will take. Responding to emails, writing an article, parent-teacher meetings, my book club, going for a run: I can't seem to get it all done in one day.

I'm not the only one who has the feeling of constantly lacking time. It is a typical feature of our modern lives. German philosopher and author Rüdiger Safranski says that adults have actually gained more free time, but we don't seem to be capable of managing our time well. According to Safranski, the percentage of time that could qualify as free time is increasing, but it is mainly spent watching TV or surfing the Internet, and is dictated by the rhythm of time that dominates these media. Instead of going to bed early with a book, we watch our favorite Netflix series and get so wrapped up in the shows that we think, *Okay, just one more episode.*

OWN-TIME

It's usually during my vacations that I'm most in tune with myself. That feeling of having too little time suddenly evaporates. I don't put any demands on myself and don't overplan my days. My phone is turned off and my TV and laptop are at home. Safranski calls this "internal time." It's something we can experience when we have the opportunity to move away from the concept of how the general public defines time.

One vacation that I sometimes look back on with a sense of nostalgia was when we stayed at a campsite in southern Italy. We had been invited by a group of Italian friends who took turns cooking dinner. Because I don't speak Italian, we couldn't communicate much. Our days there were dictated by the rhythm of the meals. A day at the campsite seemed endless, but I never got bored. I felt like I was living in a bubble of timelessness. My main activity consisted of waiting on the beach until the meal was ready. I had never come home from a vacation so well-rested.

IT'S YOUR CHOICE

In the day-to-day merry-go-round of available hours, it's all about the ways you choose to spend your time.

Alex Soojung-Kim Pang, the author of *Rest: Why You Get More Done When You*

Past, present, and future don't exist, per se. They are all present in the mind.

Work Less, says that when it comes to creative work, we actually get much more done when we do focused work for a short period of time and then structure time off for rest and reflection. In an interview with American author and host of the *Hurry Slowly* podcast, Jocelyn K. Glei, Pang says that the greatest minds usually work a four-hour workday, and that they cultivate leisure so that their minds have time to process the focused work.

When you look at it objectively, there is no such thing as too little time. An hour always lasts sixty minutes; there has never been an hour that only has forty or fifty minutes. In other words, a shortage of time is actually about something else—making better or different use of the available time.

SWITCHING GEARS

Dr. Stephan Rechtschaffen, cofounder of the Omega Institute for Holistic Studies and author of *Time Shifting: Creating More Time to Enjoy Your Life*, writes that we all know, intuitively, that time bends depending on what's happening in our lives. "Some days are long, some short; some minutes go by like an hour; some hours like a minute. You meet an old friend and wonder where the years have gone since your last meeting, and sometimes it seems you've never parted and time hasn't interfered with your feelings of friendship."

In his book, *Why Time Flies: A Mostly Scientific Investigation*, American writer Alan Burdick explores a similar notion, pointing out

that as early as the fourth century, the Roman-African philosopher St. Augustine of Hippo found that what we call three tenses are actually only one: "Past, present and future don't exist per se," writes Burdick. "They are *all* present in the mind—in our current memory of past events, in our current attention to the present, and in our current expectation of what's to come."

In other words, we are always in the present moment; the future and the past don't exist except in the fact that we're thinking about them. So maybe if we make the most of the present moment, allow it to last a little bit, the past and the future will seem to have expanded, too.

LESS PRODUCTIVE

So time is a question of perception and feeling, and Rechtschaffen suggests that the feeling of "too little time" comes from the idea that our value as people is linked, in this modern world, to our productivity: The more we get accomplished, the better we are. "I'm so busy" has become a way of boasting. If that's our approach to our lives, nothing we do is ever really making us feel like we've done enough with the time we have. Rechtschaffen writes that, to give us a sense that time is on our side, we should choose activities that we might think are just "unproductive."

Listening to some peaceful music between tasks, daydreaming, leaving work early sometimes without any particular agenda in mind, looking out the window and watching the birds, walking in the woods, or doing some gardening are perfect ways to open up space in your mind, to connect with nature, and to feel a sense of timelessness all around you. It's all about allowing yourself to "reset to a relaxed rhythm," which will ultimately help open up space and time in our daily lives.

When characterizing the process of time-shifting, Rechtschaffen uses the analogy of a bike. "Timeshifting leads us to shifting our rhythm to join the external rhythm of the moment, or to tuning into our own rhythm and choosing to stay with it," he writes. "Unfortunately, most of the time, without awareness of the rhythm of the moment, we are just swept along, marching to the beat around us. [. . .] Timeshifting, like shifting the gears on a bicycle, is finding the pace of everyday life most deeply nourishing to our soul as well as completing the myriad tasks and responsibilities at hand. In order to live well in modern society, we must be able to switch rhythms effectively throughout the day."

LOW GEAR

I often find myself secretly looking for that simplicity and the elusive lower gear; back to a time that doesn't move as fast as I do. I occasionally manage to achieve or experience one of these moments, like recently, when I was camping at the edge of a forest and I heard the high-pitched call of an owl. The call, to me, was an indication of timelessness: This is what it has always done and there will always be owls that make this sound. This made me realize how I am just a minuscule piece in the immense concept of time. It's a good way to put the breakneck pace of our lives into perspective.

WANT TO KNOW MORE?

- Hurryslowly.co is a podcast by Jocelyn K. Glei about how you can be more productive, creative, and resilient by slowing down.

- *Rest: Why You Get More Done When You Work Less* by Alex Soojung-Kim Pang

- *Time Shifting: Creating More Time To Enjoy Your Life* by Dr. Stephan Rechtschaffen

- *Why Time Flies: A Mostly Scientific Investigation* by Alan Burdick

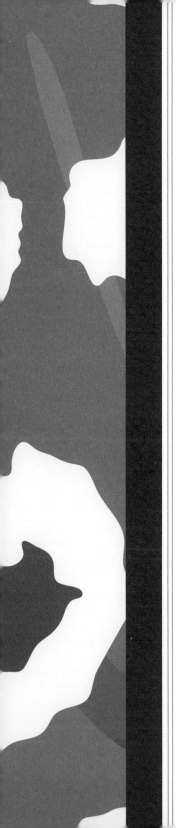
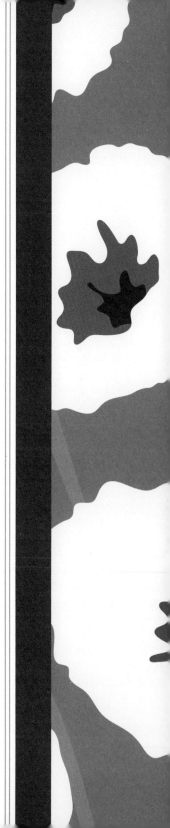

Chapter 6

LOVE YOUR UPS AND DOWNS

SOME PERIODS IN LIFE ARE TRANSITIONAL. When a child moves on to a new chapter in their own life (Astrid), it ushers in a new stage in your life, too. Or when a relationship is in turmoil (Irene). Or big changes are afoot at work (both of us). There are countless situations in which we find ourselves dealing with change, and we don't always like them. It's hard to stay calm in stormy weather, and not responding well can sometimes make us feel even worse.

It's easy to envy those who seem less affected by change—we admire how they seem to be able to stay calm amid the chaos and secure in their knowledge that everything will work out. Deep in our hearts maybe we know that, too, but we still feel unsettled during big changes.

We've come to realize that there is actually a kind of beauty to these shaky times, because these are the periods in which we learn the most about life. We focus on who we are and why we are the way we are. We get in touch with our feelings, delving into hidden recesses to find out what we're truly looking for or want—and what we expect or where we're going.

And when the storm has passed, life feels exceptionally rich. Everything is securely in its place again and we can revel in the peace and quiet—until the next storm, that is. Dutch author Griet Op de Beeck expresses this as embracing intensity, which "allows the dreadful and the beautiful to live together side by side."

A DIFFERENT KIND OF HAPPINESS

=== **BY OTJE VAN DER LELIJ** ===

*If we are continuously searching for happiness,
we often end up feeling dissatisfied and lost.
But going with the flow of life is what it's all about.*

I'd just finished reading *Brave New World*, the famous science-fiction novel from 1932 by British author Aldous Huxley. In the dystopian society that Huxley describes, happiness is used as a weapon, as an instrument to keep the people pacified. After all, satisfied and happy people do not rise in rebellion. So people in the book are encouraged to enjoy themselves as much as possible, to indulge in food, sex, and buying stuff. Anything that can cause grief, fear, discomfort, or confusion has been banished from society. People live in "blissful" ignorance, and if something goes wrong they can take *soma*—a happiness-triggering narcotic with no side effects. What a dismal specter, I thought: A world that is obsessed with enjoyment and happiness, without suffering or processing emotions, is horrifyingly banal. Yet the parallels with present times are hard to ignore. Why are we so obsessed with being happy and proving it to others via the images we share on social media? Wouldn't it be a relief if we didn't have to chase happiness all the time?

ENTITLED TO HAPPINESS

As happiness and the pursuit of it has become a goal in itself, we've also started to believe that we are entitled to it. Marketing eagerly encourages a consumerist impulse. Coaches and motivational speakers seem to preach the gospel of happiness, telling us that we, too, can achieve it if we go to a workshop or read a book. Herman Pleij, professor emeritus of medieval Dutch literature at the University of Amsterdam, believes that the marketing of happiness has brought with it a certain devaluation of the concept. Happiness has become something to own, something that you can buy. And a person who is unable to achieve constant happiness is seen as a loser.

UNPLEASANTNESS INCLUDED

The problem with the word "happiness" is that everyone uses it to mean different things. Happiness can refer to a breath of fresh air, a good glass of wine, or beautiful music—an unmanageably broad concept, Pleij believes. It expands in all directions, prostitutes itself in advertising, and is packaged as an attraction everybody can afford.

Happiness has become such a broad concept, that it's difficult to have a meaningful conversation about it. Because what are we really talking about? It can simply mean happiness, but just as well may refer to a very personal experience that can hardly be expressed in words. How do we bring back more specific meaning to this happiness free-for-all? According to Australian social psychologist Brock Bastian, many people pursue superficial pleasures in their search for happiness. "We are always looking for our next purchase, our next vacation, our next feel-good experience," he says. "In the meantime, we try to fight off bad feelings as much as possible, because feeling rotten doesn't fit into our collective idea of a happy life." But this narrow approach to pursuing happiness misses the mark because our highest high points can only be achieved if we are willing to fully embrace our lowest lows.

Happiness and pain go together. When we no longer give unpleasant feelings any room in our existence, life becomes flat and meaningless.

When we no longer give unpleasant feelings any room in our existence, life becomes flat and meaningless.

LIVING IN YOUR HEAD

There is another reason why we should not be afraid of (emotional) pain: It makes us more resilient. "Compare it to a vaccination," Bastian says. "We vaccinate our children to make them immune to certain diseases, and similarly pain and stress offer a psychological vaccination against future pain and stress." In a nutshell, we would be better equipped to live our lives well if we let ourselves feel the whole range of emotions.

I recently discovered firsthand how painful experiences don't bring only bad things. I was on a hike with my partner and our daughters when our eldest daughter fell and knocked her head on a stone. She had a cut near her eyebrow and was bleeding profusely. On the way to the hospital, I thought: Okay, this, too, is life. It wasn't fun at all, but it was meaningful. There was pain, sadness, and insecurity, but also consolation, solidarity, gratitude (it could have been worse), and support. Moments when life hurts make you realize what's truly important again, for a time.

American philosopher and Harvard professor Robert Nozick also questions whether happiness really should be our highest goal. Imagine, Nozick wrote, that we could live in a happiness machine in which we could have any experience we wished for: being a pop star, writing a bestseller, being happy for a lifetime with our loved ones. While this wonderful life takes place in your head, you just lie on your own in a tank connected to equipment. If happiness is the most important thing in life, we would, in large numbers, choose to be in that machine, Nozick believes. Yet people who are asked to imagine this always choose reality, in which they have to deal with suffering, grief, and loss, and have to work hard for their happiness. I wouldn't get into a machine like that for all the happiness in the world. I want to be useful for other people and leave a beautiful planet behind for the next generation when I go. Reality is hard sometimes, but at least it's authentic and challenging.

HAVING A PURPOSE

Happiness, in the sense of enjoying things as much as possible, gives little satisfaction in the long run, according to a study that Iranian-American psychologist Emily Esfahani Smith describes in her book, *The Power of Meaning*. A research team instructed a group of college students to pursue either "meaning" or "happiness" for ten days. The students who focused on meaningful activities did things such as forgiving a friend, studying, reflecting on their values, and cheering other people up. Those who were told to pursue happiness spent their time sleeping in, playing games, shopping, or eating candy. Subjects from the happiness group had more positive feelings than the other group immediately after the experiment. But three months later, that mood boost had faded. The subjects who had focused on meaningful activities, however, felt more enriched, inspired, and like they were "part of something bigger." Esfahani Smith writes, "Their work shows that the search for meaning is far more fulfilling than the pursuit of personal happiness, and it reveals how people can go about finding meaning in their lives."

I read a while back that bringing up children diminishes people's happiness. I had to think about this rather disconcerting conclusion—it caused me to reflect on how I experienced becoming a parent. I found the first years of parenting quite hard and sometimes quite boring. Getting out of bed three times a night, changing diapers, endlessly cleaning up toys, working fulltime during the day, keeping up with the housework. At times I felt very somber, because I didn't know how to manage it all. And yet, though raising small children didn't always fill each moment with a joyful, mood-boosting kind of happiness, it is still the best thing that has happened to me. Motherhood has given my life direction and depth. And ultimately—in my view—more happiness.

IT'S NOT ALL ABOUT PLEASURE

Thijssen thinks that suffering and happiness can coexist perfectly. You can feel down and still be happy. "The big misunderstanding in today's world is that people confuse happiness with pleasure," he says. "There is nothing wrong with enjoying things, but it is something essentially different than actually being happy. Enjoyment is temporary and is caused by things from the outside. You can enjoy a delicious meal, a good movie, a promotion at work, or a pair of new shoes. But at a certain moment that feeling wears away. Happiness is much more stable and has to do with a lifestyle, finding a spiritual balance in which you will flourish." The interpretation of happiness that Thijssen likes is based on an old philosophical theory, which revolves around one question:

"Happiness is like a butterfly. the more you chase it, the more it will evade you, but if you notice the other things around you, it will gently come and sit on your shoulder."

–Henry David Thoreau (1817-1862)

We rarely get what we want, and we get a lot of things that we don't want.

What is actually a good life, and therefore a happy life? Philosophers felt that it had nothing to do with the base pursuit of pleasure. It is about moderation, humanity, and love—and also justice, courage, and purpose.

Feelings and moods come and go (Are you having a bad day? Perhaps your relationship ended or you lost your job.) but, according to Thijssen, do not have to affect our happiness. The big question is: How do you deal with the things that happen to you? Because that's where you can make a difference. Thijssen explains, "We often let ourselves be carried away by the emotions we feel in response to unpleasant events. We can also learn to take a step back and to ask ourselves: Is my interpretation of the situation correct? Is this job really so desirable? Does this person really want to hurt me? We can reevaluate the ways we react."

MEDLEY OF HAPPINESS

By incorporating such a moment of reflection, you stay one step ahead of your impulses, defeating the patterns that no longer serve you, and consciously choosing how you want to react. And that's how, according to Thijssen, you will eventually become happier—yes, happier. That requires practice; it is not a quick fix and you can't buy it in the store. It's an attitude to life that you have to keep working on. The medley of happiness that Pleij talks about is full of different interpretations and approaches,

it turns out. Bastian believes that we can only find true happiness if we become less rigid in our dealings with (emotional) pain. According to Esfahani Smith, it's better for us to focus more on finding purpose. And Thijssen thinks that purpose is an integral part of the happiness concept. I don't know what I think yet. Maybe more than anything, we should keep having good conversations about it until deep into the night—with people we like to see, and with whom we can cry and be sad, too. That's what happiness is for me: feeling connected, having a purpose—and, sometimes, letting go.

WANT TO KNOW MORE?

- *The Other Side of Happiness: Embracing a More Fearless Approach to Living* by Brock Bastian

- *The Power of Meaning: Crafting a Life That Matters* by Emily Esfahani Smith

My Own User Manual

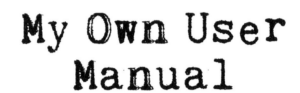

=== **BY BARBARA TAMMES** ===

Getting to know yourself isn't easy,
but if you're willing to sit down and give it
some thought, it will help you learn about yourself
and remind you what you need. If you choose,
you can even share your personal user manual
with others—it's self-knowledge in your pocket!

HOW DO YOU DO IT?

BY CATELIJNE ELZES

*Liking yourself more, or at least putting yourself down less,
is possible to do, even if it involves a bit of trial and error.*

All in all, I think I'm a pretty friendly person. I'm open and even funny on occasion. But if something goes wrong, if I make a mistake or clash with someone, a tough side of me comes out—a strict schoolteacher type who would love to rap me on the knuckles with her ruler. She's incapable of saying anything nice, and it throws me off balance, making me unsure which way to turn or what to do.

American writer and associate professor at the University of Texas at Austin Kristin Neff has been researching self-compassion for years. One of her studies has shown that for an amazing 78 percent of people, it's easier to be kind and understanding to someone other than themselves. Only 2 percent of people have more compassion for themselves than for others and 20 percent show the same amount of compassion for themselves as they do for others.

Dutch mindfulness and self-compassion trainer Marlou Kleve sees this a lot during her training courses: people who are too hard on themselves if, in their eyes, they have failed.

SELF-PROTECTION

To show how hard we can sometimes be on ourselves, Kleve often has her students do the following exercise: Imagine that a good friend is struggling with something. They have forgotten an important work appointment, for example. What would you say or do? Write this down in a few sentences, and then describe how you would react if something similar happened to you. "The difference between what people tell themselves and what they say to someone else

is so completely different," Kleve says. "To a good friend, they would say something along these lines: 'Oh, that's a shame. It happens though; we've all done it.' They usually give a tip on how to prevent something like this from happening again in the future. But when it comes to themselves, they see a loser. They put themselves down, really beat themselves up about it. 'How could you be so stupid?' And they are still angry at themselves hours later.

"This critical voice is not all bad; it can also serve a purpose," Kleve explains. "It's in our genes. It is trying to protect you, ensure that you survive. Missing an important meeting can be an intimidating experience. If it happens too often, you could lose your job. In order to ensure that you never forget a meeting again, you give yourself a lashing. The critical voice wants to protect you, but is often far from constructive. Repetitive, harsh self-criticism can lead to less self-confidence and a fear of failure. The compassion in our responses to good friends who make a mistake works better in the long run. It's just harder to do ourselves the same courtesy. We are trapped in an instinctive response to danger—we get stressed and start lashing out. At times like this, it helps to imagine how a good friend would respond. And then to tell yourself what they would tell you."

KNOW WHAT YOU ARE FEELING

I take Kleve's advice and do a "What-would-X-say?" exercise now and then. I'm lucky to have a good friend who always has words of wisdom for me when I'm struggling. Thinking of the words she would use really helps me to calm down or stay calm, and not judge myself too harshly. Recently, my bike got stolen because I forgot to lock it. My friend, of course, noted what a shame it was but that I *had* been really busy lately, and reminded me "that's when you forget things." And, "Ultimately, it really is the thief's fault. It's your bike!" Something else that helps is laying my hand on my stomach (or arm or shoulder or heart), another tip from Kleve. I can observe what I'm feeling. What am I afraid of? Which thoughts are playing tricks on me? According to Neff, this form of awareness is

TAMING THE MONKEY

American writer and former advertising executive Danny Gregory uses the metaphor of a monkey on your shoulder in his book, *Shut Your Monkey: How to Control Your Inner Critic and Get More Done*. One of the monkeys that he has invented is the Worrier, which pushes us to worry as much as possible: "Look, just be anxious. Because if you worry about absolutely everything, at least you are prepared for the inevitable disaster." Another monkey is the Lug, the one whispering in your ear to just give up: "Let's forget it. Come curl up in a ball on the couch, watch *Judge Judy* and empty another quart of Chunky Monkey ice cream." According to Gregory, you can start taming the monkey by peeling away the layers and figuring out what exactly is behind its words. What underlying fear does your monkey represent? "Peel the onion," Gregory says. "Once you know this, you'll know what you have to do."

The fact that you can bring more joy to the world by taking good care of yourself was a real eye-opener for me.

Before I know it, there's a monkey on my shoulder, jumping up and down and crying out, *That's why you shouldn't be so argumentative with clients!* and *Be happy that you have work!* or *Please restrain yourself next time!* If I sit down to really feel what's wrong, I feel the fear of being rejected, of getting less work, getting a reputation as being labeled "difficult." But there's also pride. I stood up for what I wrote. Maybe I didn't do it in the most gracious way possible, but then again, it's not like I do this all the time.

TAKING CARE OF YOURSELF

According to Kleve, the automatic question that follows "What am I feeling?" is "What do I need right now?" It might all seem a bit ego-centric because it means only focusing on yourself, but Kleve disputes this wholeheartedly. "You can't be there for someone else unless you have first taken care of yourself in the right way," she says. "When things are going well for you, you have more to give. Research conducted at the University of Groningen in the Netherlands confirms this: People who love themselves are capable of more feelings of love and passion for someone else."

What you need depends on the moment and your personality. Sometimes simply

indispensable if you want to be kinder to yourself. Or, as Kleve says, "Calmly observing your thoughts, feelings, and physical sensations puts you in touch with your emotions and your body, and enables you to allow things to be what they are. This is necessary; if you don't even notice your own pain or don't allow yourself to be affected by your emotions because you are suppressing or ignoring them, you won't realize that you need self-compassion." Besides, she explains, this form of awareness creates distance between you and your experiences. And we need this distance; if we are completely overwhelmed by pain and sadness, we won't be able to practice self-compassion.

I got a real taste of this for myself after a run-in with a client. In an email, she tells me that she thinks I'm hard to get along with.

Just try again tomorrow. You always have a second chance. And a third.

naming your pain or expressing a wish to yourself can help. You can also try a breathing exercise: Exhale your stress and inhale comfort, support, strength, or calm. "You might feel the need to go drink coffee with a friend, take a long bath, or go for a walk," Kleve says. "The things that nourish you at a time like this are what you need."

In general, it is important to continue to allow yourself to enjoy certain things in order to be able to remain compassionate, for yourself but also for others. Kleve has created a list of things you can do for your body and mind. Examples include exercise or cooking a delicious and healthy treat for yourself, giving yourself a foot massage, buying yourself flowers, drawing, watching an interesting documentary, and learning how to surf. Focusing on positive events, big and small successes, and personal victories also helps. Kleve also mentions things you can do to continue to feel connected to others, such as offering your help, smiling at people on the street, and greeting your coworkers cheerfully even if you're having a rotten day.

SECOND CHANCE

Going easier on yourself takes practice. It's a new habit, a new way of looking at things, and this takes time. In addition to asking yourself "What would a good friend say?" things like feeling what there is to feel and telling someone about it or writing it down also help. The fact that I can bring more joy to the world by taking good care of myself was a real eye-opener for me. I recently applied this technique when I woke up one Monday morning after a weekend of crying, and feeling overwhelmed. I put my sunglasses on, grabbed my bag, and spent the entire morning at a café, sitting on the terrace outside by the water, reading a magazine. I should have been working, but this was something I obviously needed. And it's true: Because I took a break, I felt much better afterward and that afternoon, it was easier to be nicer to my kids, the neighbor, and strangers at the supermarket.

Another thing that really helped me was realizing that a strict schoolteacher in your head or a monkey on your shoulder trying to get your attention are not necessarily bad things. As the American writer Danny Gregory (author of *Shut Your Monkey*, see sidebar on page 172) writes, the monkey is part of what has made you *you*. Don't try to surgically remove him from your head or to delete him entirely; just don't allow him to control your life.

And if the monkey or schoolteacher has hold of the reins now and then, go easy on yourself. Just try again tomorrow. You always have a second chance. And a third, and a hundredth. Remember where it all started: Being less hard on yourself.

ROLL NOTES ⟶

Use the notes on the following page as a reminder to go easier on yourself. Cut them out, curl them up into a spiral, place them in a jar or bowl, and pull one out every now and then to read.

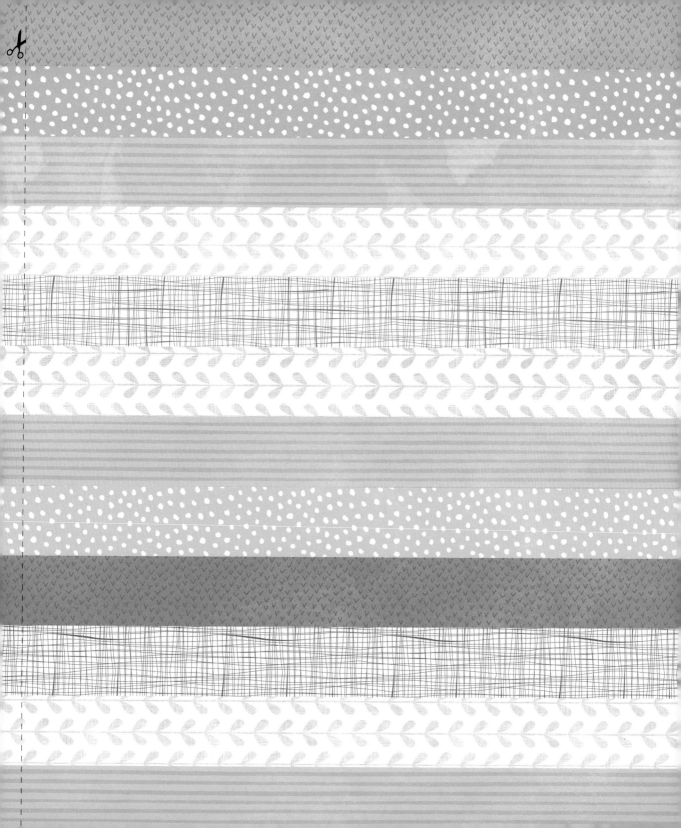

•●• Making time for a walk is a good idea. ○●○

 What a perfect day for an off-day.

For today: Buy fresh flowers (and create your own pretty bouquet).

"Mistakes are lessons in disguise."
—Danny Gregory

 Sports or exercise are also good for the mind.

Time you enjoyed wasting is not wasted time.

"There is more to life than increasing its speed."
—Mahatma Gandhi

 Who says you have to do it?

Just hang in there a little longer; it will be okay.

"If you wouldn't say it to a friend, don't say it to yourself."
—Jane Travis

Today I put myself first.

✦✦✦ I don't always have to fix everything (by myself). ✦✦✦

Why wait till tomorrow?

=== BY CAROLYN BUIJS ===

*Making something, doing something,
taking an action you wouldn't ordinarily take . . .
Here are some prompts you can try when you
feel like shaking things up.*

Stick a postcard here that matches your mood today.

1

```
     `    ⁄
   ⁻ GLUE ⁻
     HERE ⁻
   ⁄        ⁓
        ∖
```

2 Fold and cut out a tiny snowflake from a colorful piece of paper. Stick it here.

3

Make a flower out of everyday materials: newspaper, packaging, wrapping paper, etc. "Plant" your flower here.

4 Open an atlas, pick a random destination, and write three lines about what you think it looks like there.

- -

- -

- -

5 Draw your lunch.

Cut out a piece of text from a
newspaper or magazine, stick it here,
and circle the words that you like.
Or make the other words illegible. **6**

7

Take a photo of the same place at the same time every day for a week (for example, the street where you live) and stick your photos here.

MONDAY

TUESDAY

FRIDAY

WEDNESDAY

THURSDAY

SATURDAY

SUNDAY

Draw a pretty sign.

 Draw your cat (or google an image of a cat and draw that).

10 Draw your kitchen counter: before and after cooking.

11 Cut a rabbit silhouette out of a piece of paper. Stick it in here.

Ask someone to draw a scribble or line. Now you turn that into a drawing.

12

13

Ask someone
to write a
word. Now
turn it into a
small poem.

NOTICE ALL THAT IS GOOD

BY MARIJE VAN DER HAAR-PETERS

Deep down we all know that happiness can be found in simple and everyday things, yet we tend to overlook them because we're just too busy. But when we write down those little moments of joy, we start to notice them more often.

There is plenty of scientific evidence to show that reflecting on the little things you are grateful for is not only fun, but also beneficial. For example, it seems that gratitude gives rise to behavior that we regard as moral and good. Grateful people are more caring, more compassionate and fair, and have more respect for others. Robert Emmons, gratitude expert and professor of psychology at the University of California, Davis, believes gratitude boosts energy and inspiration. "Gratitude provides life with meaning by encapsulating life itself as a gift," he writes. By focusing on what you *do* have instead of what you don't, you can generate feelings of happiness and comfort during difficult times. Give yourself a boost of gratitude by filling in the prompts on the next two pages.

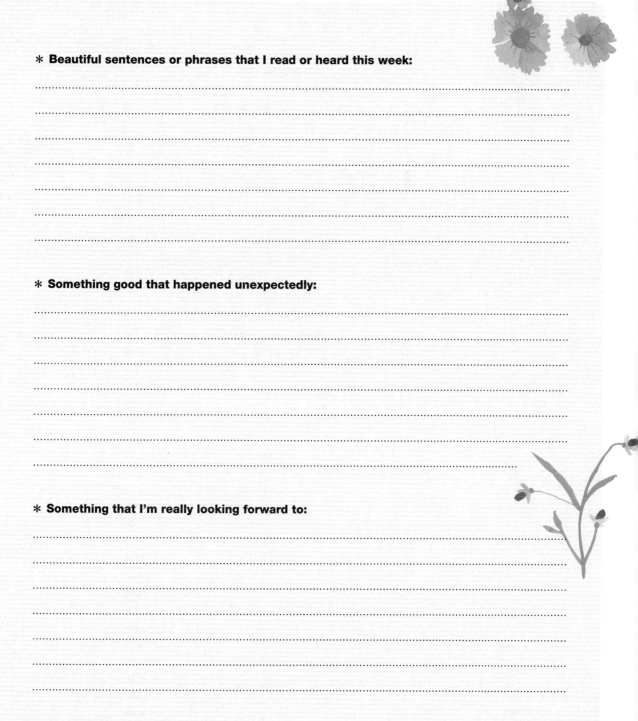

✳ Beautiful sentences or phrases that I read or heard this week:

....

....

....

....

....

....

....

✳ Something good that happened unexpectedly:

....

....

....

....

....

....

....

✳ Something that I'm really looking forward to:

....

....

....

....

....

....

....

* A fear I successfully overcame:

....

....

....

....

....

....

....

* A song that makes me happy:

....

....

....

....

....

....

....

* Things that worked out really well this month:

....

....

....

....

....

....

today
is for
lingering

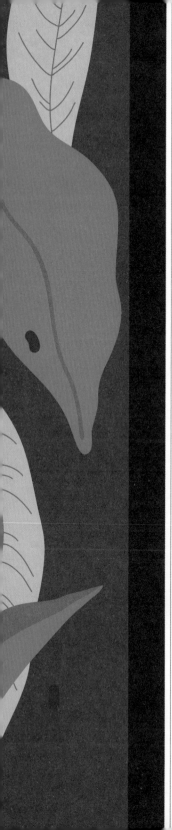

Chapter 7

LOVE LETTING GO

WE HAVE NEVER BEEN VERY GOOD AT letting go of things. Until COVID-19—that crash course in letting go—hit the world, we (Irene and Astrid) were used to living our organized lives: activities neatly arranged in schedules, with everything planned often down to the minute. Using a combination of paper planners and an online calendar, we knew what was on the horizon months in advance. It gave us the feeling that even when things were hectic, everything was wonderfully under control. But then the world changed, and it rendered our schedules and control mechanisms completely useless.

At first, this caused some struggle and upheaval. Many of those who were lucky enough not to be affected physically by the virus still suffered from anxiety and other disorders. After a few weeks, we made a conscious effort to embrace this new reality and practice the art of letting go. A few weeks after that, we felt a shift. Life began to feel much easier. And now we know that life does indeed go on, even when every moment isn't perfectly planned. We also learned that living a bit more spontaneously can be so much more worthwhile. Because when nothing is planned, we're leaving space for the most beautiful things to come our way.

ACCEPTING
AMBIGUITY

=== BY OLIVIA GAGAN ===

Modern life has little to do with subtlety and nuance. Many of us spend years thinking in black and white, but you can look at everything from multiple angles— and that realization can be truly liberating.

Have you ever tried to explain something you don't really understand? A scientific concept to a child, perhaps, or a business idea in a meeting, or the storyline of a film you only half-watched? It's hard. And you risk looking like an idiot if the person you're speaking to realizes that you have no clue what you're talking about.

When I was seventeen, I tried to explain an idea I didn't understand in an attempt to get into a prestigious university. To win a place to study English there, you have to write and submit an essay on a topic of your choice. On the day of the admissions interview, you take a timed writing test, and then you're interviewed by a panel of academics about your essay. It's a rigorous process.

I didn't know what to write about in my essay. I wondered what would impress the academics the most. I did know that I loved the writer F. Scott Fitzgerald and had devoured his books, letters, and essays over the preceding year. With the deadline looming, my teacher suggested I write about one of the celebrated American author's most famous quotes: "The test of a first-rate intelligence is the ability to hold two opposed ideas in mind at the same time and still retain the ability to function."

I didn't tell my teacher that I couldn't wrap my mind around the quote. In my essay, I tried to logically explain why it's possible to think two things at once, but really, I had no idea what Fitzgerald was saying. How does living with two opposing things at once make you clever? I wrote the essay, feeling all the while deeply unsure of myself.

Fast-forward a few months, to the day of the interview, and my shaky essay was put to the test. I sat in a dark, wood-paneled room, waiting to be called on. It was like stepping back in time: The centuries-old university was fairy-tale–like down to its creaking staircases and medieval walls. Nervously awaiting my slot, I could hear the candidate before me laughing and chatting with the interviewers. She floated out and breathed "You'll love it!" to me as I walked, terrified, into the room.

> By deciding that you don't need to know exactly what something or somebody is about, you create room for life and people and places to surprise you.

I did not love it. For the next twenty minutes, two academics interrogated me on exactly what I meant by my essay. In what I now recognize as a textbook good-cop-bad-cop routine, one picked holes in everything I'd written, while the other offered positive feedback.

Here was a Fitzgerald-style test playing out right in front of me. One person was saying my work was good, another person was saying it was not. I had no idea what to do. Agree with both of them? Try and answer them one at a time? My brain felt overloaded. Cheeks burning, I mumbled incoherently, confused, wrong-footed. I had failed Fitzgerald's test of intelligence. A university-stamped rejection letter dropped on my doormat soon after.

BLACK-AND-WHITE THINKING

That essay was the first sign that I'm not very good at accepting more than one version of events, of what Fitzgerald called "holding two opposed ideas in mind at the same time." Ambiguity—defined as the ability to be uncertain, to be open to more than one interpretation or one reason for things—is not my cup of tea.

I like things to be certain. In the past, I've tended to categorize people as "goodies" or "baddies." Experiences—a relationship, a holiday, a meal—are also remembered as either good or bad. I like feeling sure of things. I like clear, predictable patterns and rules. When a "maybe" happens that threatens my certainty, I feel uncomfortable, unsafe, and let down.

It's not just me; modern life, it turns out, doesn't like nuance either. Social media in particular is a place where things are increasingly black and white—we see either the highlight reel of each other's lives, or our worst, angriest rants. Political views are polarized. There's no room for debate, evolving feelings, or being uncertain.

Scrolling through my feed once, I saw this play out in real time. One post read, "I hate this [expletive] country, honestly. I know we're supposed to love it, but at a certain point you have to look around and see what it actually is." Immediately underneath this message, another person posted, "The Earth is [expletive] beautiful." Both views were so over-the-top, so extreme that it made me laugh out loud. Both people were screaming into the online abyss, convinced they were right.

OPPOSING IDEAS

The desire to label things as right or wrong isn't a new phenomenon confined to social media, however—it is simply amplified by it. Philosophers have grappled with accepting ambiguity for thousands of years. From Socrates to Simone de Beauvoir, people have spent millennia trying to figure out if—and how—two opposing things can be true at once. Psychologists argue that the human brain inherently struggles to juggle opposing ideas. We're hardwired to seek certainty, to find absolute truth. This quest for certainty has no doubt helped drive our evolution—the desire to know, to understand, is at the very root of all human advancement. But nevertheless, it seems we can't be certain and have a perfect explanation for everything.

I haven't devoted as much study to it as the philosophers, but everyday life has shown me that things are not always black or white. When a short romantic relationship ended suddenly, for instance, I was upset that he wanted instead to focus on his work and pursue other people. I immediately wanted to write him off as a "baddie." But as I processed the relationship, I also recognized that he was the most mature and kind person I'd ever dated. We hadn't lasted long, but he'd made a big positive impact on me. Ergo, a relationship that turned sour nevertheless held many positive elements. And if you asked him about his experience of us being together, I'm sure it would sound quite different to mine—and yet both experiences, both recollections, would be true.

DIFFERENT FROM ME

Friendships have also chipped cracks into my ability to be absolutely sure about everything and everyone. I've shared wonderful memories with some people I've grown up with, but over the years, sometimes I realize that our values aren't the same. They make decisions I wouldn't make. Does this make them bad? No. It just makes them different from me. How will my friendships evolve? Will we remain friends?

Right now, I don't know. I have to learn to live with the uncertainty until I find out.

As a teenager, when I first tried to understand Fitzgerald's quote, I hadn't yet had the experiences I needed to understand the concept of ambiguity. My romantic relationships and my friendships have both since taught me that the most well-meaning people can do unexpected or hurtful things. Even more confusingly, people that seem unpleasant can show occasional flashes of kindness and helpfulness. I now understand that someone can be hardworking but occasionally very lazy. A great listener, but sometimes selfish. A loyal friend, but an unfaithful romantic partner. The funniest person in the room may also be the saddest one.

LIVING WITH UNCERTAINTY

I have become kinder by being willing to accept that not everyone (including myself) will behave predictably all the time. Some might call it learning to live with ambiguity, but I think it can also be called growing up. I think my former need for things to be black or white was, in part, about control, something to cling to in an unpredictable, volatile world. But people do unexpected, wonderful things, forcing you to rewrite your ideas about them. A secret comes to light that shows someone in a whole new light.

Sticking to my fixed ideas was also arrogant. Who am I to decide who someone is or isn't? I'm not a fixed, unchanging person. I have evolved considerably over the years. I've

> The human brain inherently struggles to juggle opposing ideas. We're hardwired to seek certainty.

become better at some things, and I've left some bad habits behind (while no doubt picking up a few new ones along the way). Why can't others be allowed to grow and change and do the same?

Examining my need for certainty has highlighted my own weaknesses. I've tended to end contact with people after they've hurt me—after I have written them off as bad news. Shouldn't I be questioning where I contributed to the problem, too? Isn't it just as cruel to discard someone for one false step? I'm not sure. And I'm okay with that.

RELINQUISHING CONTROL

Learning to tolerate ambiguity, being able to hold two opposing ideas in my mind at the same time, has made me calmer and happier. It's meant relinquishing control and admitting I don't know all the answers. It's humbling and, in a strange way, liberating.

Because by deciding that you don't need to know exactly what something or somebody is about, you create room for life and people and places to surprise you. When you're open-minded to a range of different possibilities and interpretations and outcomes, you see more, experience more, feel more. Wanting things to be certain is a bit of a fool's errand. It can hold you back from making commitments and trusting people. Accepting uncertainty is a matter of having faith. Not necessarily the religious kind, but the kind that admits we don't have all the answers.

Simone de Beauvoir advised that when hungering for the very human desire for certainty, simply accepting that life is essentially uncertain can set us free. "Since we do not succeed in fleeing it, let us, therefore, try to look the truth in the face," she wrote. "Let us try to assume our fundamental ambiguity. It is in the knowledge of the genuine conditions of our life that we must draw our strength to live and our reason for acting." In the face of *many* ideas potentially being true, I think she's advocating for us all finding our own personal reasons for living, seeking our own personal truths and creeds, which, if we're kind, can peacefully coexist with one another's.

Do I understand that Fitzgerald quote now? I think I do. Or at least, I have my own take on it. I now believe that what I should have done in that interview with the academics was to defend my writing, my unique point of view. That's what they were interested in. I understand that now; I just didn't when I was seventeen.

So, this piece is my second attempt at that entrance exam. I wonder if I'd have had a better chance at getting in this time around.

WANT TO READ MORE?
- *The Crack-Up* by F. Scott Fitzgerald
- *The Ethics of Ambiguity* by Simone de Beauvoir

you CAN'T CONTROL everything

— JULES EVANS

A LITTLE DOUBT IS GOOD FOR YOU

BY OTJE VAN DER LELIJ

Most of us believe that confidence is a strength, if not a virtue.
But entertaining strong doubts about yourself has surprising benefits, too.
Let's investigate the positive side of human insecurity.

Brilliant, but deeply insecure about his talent: that was Vincent van Gogh, now one of the world's most recognized and revered painters. How could such a talented person, who painted such stunning landscapes, self-portraits, and sunflowers, have suffered from self-doubt? And yet, as shown in the book *Ever Yours: The Essential Letters*, which features hundreds of Van Gogh's letters, he did. When art critic Albert Aurier wrote a favorable review in a leading art magazine, praising the artist, Van Gogh was uncomfortable with the flattery. He even wrote a letter to the critic to say that Aurier described beautifully what he would have liked to have achieved, but that there was only one artist deserving of such praise: the French painter Paul Gauguin. Van Gogh also dismissed other expressions of admiration for his work. For his entire life, he continued to have deep doubts about his own abilities.

STEADFAST COMPETITION

"Insecurity, self-doubt: It's all part of being human," says Dutch psychologist and author Robert Haringsma. "Life is, by definition, a rather insecure state. You never know what tomorrow will bring. You could suddenly become very ill, or meet the love of your life. You can also never predict how other people will react to you, what they think of you, or how they value your work. I like to compare life to a game of poker: On the one hand, it depends on your own effort, and on the other, it depends on the cards you are dealt. You can certainly influence the game, but you never control it. In that sense, I believe insecurity is firmly entrenched in the human condition. There will always be insecurities, and moments when your faith in yourself and the world around you shows some cracks."

I certainly have my own set of insecurities. Want me to interview an eminent professor or celebrity? No problem. But the simple act of introducing myself to a group of strangers paralyzes me. My insecurity is also present when I'm writing, a constant companion. There is always that voice in my head saying: *You have to do better. Is this interesting enough? Will anyone really want to read this?* I know I'm not the only one who has these thoughts from time to time. I don't know anyone who doesn't. Even the people I look up to, giants in their field, can't escape it.

JUST BE YOURSELF

Insecurity is a pretty broad concept. You can be unsure of almost anything, such as your own competence: how good you are at doing something. But you can also doubt your value: whether you have a right to exist as a human; if you are good enough. Together, says Haringsma, these things form your level of self-confidence. And then there are insecurities about the future, the choices you make, the reactions of other people. Just being yourself can be a tall order.

A lot of people think insecurity is a female trait. It's hard to admit, but I can relate to that. Men seem to just open their mouths and speak, without all the anxiety about how they will appear to strangers. I see this in many of my male friends. My female friends can fret about stuff endlessly, while my male friends simply say, "Just be yourself; leave it to other people to make their mind up about you." Completely true and I agree, but it can be so hard to be yourself when you feel all eyes are on you and

Life is, by definition, a rather insecure state. You never know what tomorrow will bring.

your heart is in your mouth. I also get the feeling men are less shy about asking for a raise and that they make decisions more quickly—even when it's the wrong decision. Does that mean men have more self-confidence? "Not at all," says Haringsma. "They just deal with their insecurities differently. When women feel unsure of themselves, they take a step back, whereas men pretend everything is okay and bluff their way through, while in their hearts they are just as insecure as women."

IT HELPS TO VEER OFF COURSE

Insecurity is often viewed as a problem, something we need to overcome. Those people who seem so sure of everything, who are confident, seem to go the furthest in life. But this unjustly dismisses insecurity as an inferior value, while actually there are plenty of benefits to a good dose of self-doubt every now and then. Tomas Chamorro-Premuzic, professor of business psychology at the University College London, even says it is the less self-assured people who have the most success—people who doubt themselves and their abilities are more critical of themselves and more open to feedback than people with spades of self-confidence. What's more, they work harder and appear less arrogant: all characteristics that may not make life easier, but can lead to higher-quality results.

Many great philosophers have put forth that we should value doubt over self-assuredness. Danish-Dutch novelist and philosopher Jannah Loontjens says that Friedrich Nietzsche was one of them. "He was very much in favor of veering off course, of soul searching," Loontjens says. "We find ways to develop our thinking when we are unsure about things, and not when we are certain about everything. When in doubt, look at something from a different angle." Loontjens points out there are also contemporary philosophers who warn against so-called "sure things" because they may blind you. "They believe that you must always be suspicious of strong certainties," says Loontjens. "You must always dare to ask questions, and say 'Yes, but . . .' This leads to new insights and prevents dogmatic thinking."

DARE TO CHOOSE

Fascinated by this theme, Loontjens wrote a humorous contemporary Dutch novel about it called *Misschien wel niet* [Maybe Not]. Her main character, Mascha, is actually leading a very good life. She has a nice boyfriend, a good job, two sons, but she is unsure about everything: Is this the man I want to be with? Is this the right job for me? Am I a good mother? This causes her to lose her way, never choosing anything wholeheartedly. It gnaws at her sense of identity, and she starts feeling alienated. No matter how much Loontjens applauds the courage to feel insecure, she acknowledges that there are limits.

"When you feel that level of insecurity about your own life, it works against you," says Loontjens. "You keep floating without ever determining your own direction. It also makes it impossible to become attached to a person, because to connect with someone deeply you need to able to make choices with utter conviction. Self-doubt is good now and then, but when it becomes a chronic state, all those doubts result in superficiality. If I were to give any advice, it would be this: Dare to choose things despite all your insecurities. It gives your life more depth and meaning."

ALL DOUBTS OUT IN THE OPEN

So there is a limit to how much doubt is good. Insecurity can hold you back, but it can also be a driver for self-improvement. Where the line between the two lies exactly is different for everyone. "Insecurity is not a problem until it prevents you from reaching your goals, until it makes you suffer as a human," Haringsma says.

We are brainwashed into believing in the power of surety, of taking action. But maybe it's far more valuable to just put your doubts on the table. It not only leads to higher quality, it also takes the edge off your insecurity. Shame

Doubt helps you take someone else's viewpoint and understand how others see life.

Maybe it's far more valuable to just put your doubts on the table. It not only leads to more quality, it also takes the edge off your insecurity.

doesn't survive the spotlight, I've been told. Insecurity becomes far more bearable if you open up about it, if only to hear some other people say, "I feel the same way."

French philosopher René Descartes was good at this. "Descartes looked for very fundamental knowledge, and he did this by doubting literally everything," says Jacobs. "He began with his senses. 'Can I trust my senses? No, because they can deceive me, so I'm discounting senses as a basis of knowledge.' And he continued in that vein until only one certainty remained: the fact that he was doubting, and nobody could take that away from him."

So what should be done with all our insecurities? "First off, accept that they are part of the package of life, and also that they have a good side," Haringsma says. "If you don't accept it, you are fighting these feelings and that will only make them bigger. Don't let insecurity stop you. Take on the confrontation and make a choice, even if it makes you uncomfortable. Belgian psychiatrist Damiaan Denys said a

beautiful thing about this: 'People should try to see their fears and insecurities not as negative emotions but as opportunities.' We live in a safe cocoon in which we feel good; maybe we have a house, a partner, an income. Being really free means you dare to escape, that it's possible to take on new things that fall outside of your comfort zone." Those moments always coincide with insecurity and fear, but that's a positive thing, says Denys. "It's a sign that you are leaving a bit of yourself behind and entering a new world in which you will be challenged. It's not easy, it's painful, but you will learn from it and it can bring you a new way of looking at things."

Maybe that's why Van Gogh was such a brilliant painter, and why he had such an intelligent perspective on the world. He knew that he knew nothing for sure, he dared to doubt himself, but he also didn't let that stop him. Or in his words: "When you hear a voice within you say 'You cannot paint,' then by all means paint, and that voice will be silenced."

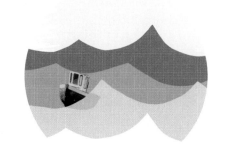

GETTING A GRIP ON THE WORLD

═ BY ANNEMIEK LECLAIRE ═

*It's easy to feel unmoored in a world
that feels so out of our control.
But there are techniques we can practice
to try to anchor our own storm-tossed ships.*

No. 32   NAME   *CARPENTER. W.*

WEEK ENDING

	HRS.	RATE	£	s	d
	38	8/9	16	12	6
	3	8/9	1	6	3
			1	7	-

TOTAL WAGES   19   5   9

INCOME TAX
INSURANCE

				5	-
			3	8	
				8	
			19		
			16	15	

SIGNATURE...

HOURS	ON.	OFF.		
8 15	7 50			
12 31	12 30			
1 29	1 30			
5 31	5 01			
		8 00		
		8 00		
9/4		3 1/4	1/4	4
		2		2
8 3/4	8	10 1/2	5	8

EC206-1   ENGLISH CLOCK SYSTEMS LAND...

At times I feel like I'm adrift in a boat on a rough sea, and the waves are too high to even think about dropping anchor. The world, and our own lives in it, can change so swiftly, and in some ways the future has never been so uncertain. Of course, parts of the planet have always had to struggle with hunger, disease, and wars. But for some time, it seemed that we were on the way up. It seemed that we had reached a place where we as a society agreed that we wanted to make life better for everyone. Political leaders were starting to work together more, minority groups were gaining rights—equal opportunities for all seemed on the horizon. But the atmosphere is changing, as is evidenced by the recent rise in popularity of political leaders who are explicit about only supporting their own group. The Israeli historian Yuval Noah Harari summarizes the disillusionment in his book *21 Lessons for the 21st Century*. "At the close of the twentieth century it appeared that the great ideological battles between fascism, communism, and liberalism resulted in the overwhelming victory of liberalism," he writes. "Democracy, human rights, and the free market seemed destined to conquer the whole world. But as always, history took an unexpected turn and, after the fall of fascism and communism, liberalism is now falling under pressure. So where are we headed?"

SOCIAL POWER

Thinkers like Harari explain the current shift towards nationalism and polarization as a social response to the increasing complexity of the world. People are looking for simple answers, they say. A simple, yet alternative way to look at things. Life in the twenty-first century is staggeringly complex, suggests writer David Christian in his book *A Big History of Everything*. We have evolved from a universe of single-celled organisms, young suns, and stars, to a world with an unbelievable quantity of knowledge, products, and possibilities that will only continue to grow. No wonder that leaders with easy-to-digest stories and platforms attract followers.

Perhaps, also, the complexity of the world is harder to stomach because we have been entertaining an exaggerated notion of our own power to change things. Is this a clash between our world-building mentality and the inevitable feelings of powerlessness we are faced with? One theory is that the generations before us were able to cope better than we did because they had less access to media. As citizens of today's world, we are consistently confronted with our powerlessness and the complexity of the world every minute of the day through the information tsunami flooding our social media and news sites. Business analysts have a name for the era we live in—VUCA: Volatile, Uncertain, Complex, and Ambiguous. VUCA means that the world is changing so quickly and in such unpredictable ways that it is very difficult for organizations to think ahead. The market, for instance, could go in any direction.

CALM IN THE STORM

You can find meditations to evoke a calm mood in apps such as Insight Timer (with categories such as Trust or Relax) or Headspace. The latter offers "Meditation for Anxiety: A 30-day Course."

I feel much calmer when I get a grip on the problem.

LOOKING FORWARD

VUCA can be applied across domains. "Uncertainty and confusion have descended upon all aspects of life," says Flemish trend-watcher Herman Konings. "In addition to political and social unrest, people's personal lives are also in flux." And though one could argue that we are all operating with a certain level of uncertainty, Konings clarifies that "the degree of uncertainty we now have is really unique." According to him, the feeling of losing one's mooring starts with our expanding opportunities—that we no longer have fixed roles in marriage, religion, education, and career means we are "able to plan our lives the way we want. But with that freedom also comes with uncertainty." As a self-employed divorcée living in a rental building where the rent is rising so fast that I won't be able to live there much longer, I know what he means. Where I'll be living in five years, and with whom, is completely unknowable. The same goes for where my children will study, or what work they'll end up doing. "Work, relationships, questions about what meaning life has, have all become [more] flexible," says Dutch philosopher Marli Huijer, and "it generates uncertainty." But it affects people navigating more traditionally stable lives, too, she notes. "The people who are still married, who have a permanent job, and [those] who have been living in the same place for years, still experience a knock-on effect of all this turbulence. Anyone who's just left their job or rents out their house through Airbnb. And all those people who change their relationship status. It also affects you. What if one of those divorced people starts to show an interest in you? It might upend your relationship. You still have to find a way to relate to all this motion around you. Even if only because you have to justify why you're not changing yourself."

According to Konings and Huijer, all the options we have available to us make it even more difficult to continue to chart our own course. Huijer says, "When I ask in a lecture hall how many students already know what they're going to do next year, only a small group raise their hands. Students just don't know yet: maybe they'll go abroad, maybe they'll start working, maybe they are going to continue their studies." There are so many possibilities.

TAKE CHARGE

That unmoored boat is also tossed in the winds of haste. According to Konings, twenty- to sixty-five-year-olds have seven fewer hours available per week than the same demographic did twenty-five years ago. We log in to work at night, or because we are stuck in a traffic jam on the way to a networking meeting, for example. This is not only at the expense of the time you need to catch your breath by visiting a friend or painting a fence, but it also gives everyone a continuous sense of being in a rush. "We are a little panicked, partly because of the constant hurrying," says Konings. "We feel as if we have no control." Taking control of what you can influence is, according to Huijer and Konings, the answer to how you can still drop an anchor on those unpredictable seas. This theory is also supported by financial analyst Carl Richards, who writes for the *New York Times* about dealing with uncertainty. He advises his readers to make a list of all the things that you *do* have influence over and then to exert that influence with small actions. "You will not have any influence on Vladimir Putin," he wrote, "but you do control how you treat your neighbor." You can take control by gathering information about issues you are concerned about. Concerning the threat of terrorism, global warming, and the effects of the robotization of the labor market, I myself feel much calmer when I have a clearer picture of what the problem is. When I can choose one of the solutions and commit to it in a way that suits me, it helps me regain my footing. So I vote for a political party that wants to look into universal basic income, I continue to choose not to own a car, and I adjust my diet so I'm not eating meat more than once a week.

Another way to get a grip on things, according to Huijer and Konings, is to determine for yourself what gives your life meaning and to live accordingly. Harari writes: "The old stories have collapsed, and no new story has yet emerged to replace them. Who are we? What should we do in life? What kind of skills do we need? Given everything we know and don't know about science, about God or gods, about politics and religion—what can we say about the meaning of life today?" I can write down my own ideas for myself: I want to be able to run my household independently, take good care of my children and other loved ones, and continue my exploration of "how to live." Living according to those priorities gives me a sense of confidence. And sensory pleasures—like dancing, walking, and eating—help ground me in the here and now.

YOUR OWN FLOTILLA

Find help and supporters, advises Huijer. She mentions initiatives by single people she knows who are making communal plans for their old age, or making the neighborhood more environmentally friendly together. The organization specialists who immerse themselves in VUCA call such a strategy "interpersonal risk taking"—which simply means seeking help at

When you go on a journey, the road appears.

—A Year with Rumi

I know that if I sink, someone will take me out of the water and carry me.

work and in other areas. *Flow* writer Caroline Buijs earlier described "finding your convoy"— a fixed group of people with whom you are on the road of life. "Flotilla" would be more appropriate for me. My boat may whirl, float, keel, and be tossed about, but the flotilla of boats surrounding me gives me the certainty that if mine sinks, someone will take me out of the water and carry me until I am ready to float again. That is very reassuring. "Seek out your friends," says Konings. "It has been proven that human contact—the human voice, the human touch—is reassuring in all sorts of ways."

Search for that connection, despite the differences, Huijer advises. At a time when people seem interested only in justifying their own perspective and calling other people snobs, naïve, or worse, it is important to keep an open attitude and to listen carefully to each other's views. Because only truly open and respectful conversation will lead to cooperation and then to peace, she says, whether it's at your kitchen table or at the government's negotiating table. VUCA specialists call this "constructive depolarization," which means: Remain calm and focus on constructive cooperation.

BREATH IN BREATH OUT

It is interesting that both Richards and Harari mention "conscious breathing" as the perfect form of support. "Just observe how everything really is right now, whatever it is," writes Harari. "When you breathe in, be aware of that: now the breath is coming in. When you exhale, be aware of that: now the breath is going out. And if your attention slips and your thoughts wander into memories and fantasies, then just be aware of that: now my thoughts have strayed from my breathing." Remarkably enough, this highly educated historian calls this "the most important thing anyone ever told me."

About the period when he lost everything due to the financial crisis, Richards writes: "The suspense was paralyzing. But I realized that while everything else may be out of control, I can control my breath. After I had done meditation exercises for a few days, I felt my sense of stability increase." So that's what I do in my little boat when the waves become too rough. I lie down and breathe in and out. And then I always reach that moment when the engine of the boat has charged enough power again to tackle the waves and get back to land. But whether it will stay there for a long time, I can't say. I love the open sea.

WANT TO READ MORE?

- *21 Lessons for the 21st Century* by Yuval Noah Harari

- *Origin Story: A Big History of Everything* by David Christian

- *A Brief History of Everyone Who Ever Lived* by Adam Rutherford

EVERYTHING WILL BE OKAY

BY MARISKA JANSEN

*Trusting that things will
be fine isn't that simple.
But it makes life so much easier.
Journalist Mariska Jansen
looks into what it takes to
maintain a trustful attitude.*

I remember saying to a friend years ago, "Just trust that it will be okay." She was sitting across from me, desperately unhappy. Her relationship had just ended and, to her, finding "the one" seemed impossible. As an outsider, it's often so much easier to see situations like these in a more positive light. In her case, it just seemed to me like a matter of time before she would find her perfect partner. And though she didn't think so that night when we were chatting on my balcony, she *did* find someone shortly after.

HOPE IS GOOD

Maintaining trust can work like a magic potion: simply by having it, we feel better. Trust means remaining confident and hopeful, despite current circumstances. My five-year-old son, for example, hadn't been showing any signs of wanting to jump into water by himself, even after having swimming lessons for a year. This lack of confidence worried me a bit, but I trusted that one day he'd overcome his fear. With his healthy little body and strong legs, it's only logical to believe that one day he'd be able to swim. According to New Zealand philosopher Annette Baier, we understand trust the same way we do clean air: We are most conscious of the air we breathe when it's scarce or impure. It's the same with trust when it's broken or lost—trust is the basis of existence and the everyday norm. We take the train and trust that we'll arrive at our destination. We drive on

the road trusting that other cars will all stay in their lane. At the same time, being trustful means accepting there is a chance, no matter how small, that the outcome will be different than what we expect. A train can malfunction, and a driver may not follow traffic rules. "Trust in things or people entails the willingness to submit to the risk that they may fail us, with the expectation that they will not, or the neglect or lack of awareness of the possibility that they might," writes Dutch author Bart Nooteboom in his book *Trust*.

VISUALIZE

How confident we feel is not only dependent on the outside world, but also on ourselves. Personally I find it difficult hanging my confidence level on the opinions of other people. My self-esteem and self-confidence sometimes take a hit due to the smallest things: Whether it is a disgruntled shop assistant, a rude waiter, or someone speaking curtly on the phone, I take it personally, and start to blame it on myself.

Confidence can be a self-fulfilling prophecy. If you set out expecting a good outcome, it will often turn out that way. On the flip side, writes Dutch author and retired professor Frans Jacobs, "Those who are scared or fearful of their future focus on the obstacles that loom before them, thereby materializing *them* into reality." How can we reassure and promise ourselves that things are going to go well? Besides visualizing positive outcomes, we also have to

trust ourselves to let go of negative thoughts. Results can be favorable even when they're not completely within our control.

KNOW YOURSELF

It is only possible to believe in yourself if you are brave enough to really get to know yourself; only then will you have the ability to overcome hardship. A lack of confidence brings about uncertainty, but too much confidence can lead to arrogance, which leads us to overestimate our abilities. Self-confidence is about having self-knowledge and using it as the basis for which you make your most important life choices: your partner(s), or job(s) you take, or where you decide to live, for example.

According to nineteenth-century American poet and thinker Ralph Waldo Emerson, we should trust our own instincts instead of concerning ourselves with what others may think. "And truly it demands something godlike in him who has cast off the common motives of humanity, and has ventured to trust himself for a taskmaster," he wrote in an essay about self-reliance.

EVERY PHASE OF LIFE IS DIFFERENT

Trust is not only about believing in yourself, but also about believing in others, even when it's possible they could let you down.

Another thing when it comes to trust is that some people base it on faith. They believe that there is a god (or gods) who watches over all things and decides fate, that whatever happens was meant to happen. Every now and then I think about something someone once told me: "We have to let go of our worries, because everything will work out in due time."

It's a comforting thought, but sometimes I wonder: *How can you trust when the hope of a good outcome seems too far-fetched?*

Maybe the meaning of being confident that everything will be okay shifts during every phase of our lives. Trust is different for a completely healthy and successful person than it is for someone who is very sick. For the latter, maybe they trust that there will be good days, that there won't be any pain, or that the doctor is doing everything they can. In every phase of life we are bound by the restrictions of reality.

What is "good" is completely different in the spring than in the fall, different at the beginning of life than it is at the end, writes Belgian philosopher and author Patricia De Martelaere. "Good is not by definition what grows, stays alive, and climbs upward," she writes. Trust also has to do with surrendering, accepting our fate, and making peace.

In the end, my friend was glad that it took her as long as it did to find "the one" because she had more time to figure out what *she* really wanted out of life. My son recently jumped into the pool all by himself—his eyes were gleaming with pride when he told me after his lesson. It made me look back at my concerns with a smile and think: *What was I so worried about?*

"WE'LL TAKE THIS LEAP AND WE'LL SEE. WE'LL JUMP AND WE'LL SEE. THAT'S LIFE."

—From the film *Joe Versus the Volcano*, quoted by Meg Ryan

INDEX

CREDITS

Editors and translators of *Flow* Magazine

Rachel Lancashire

Caroline Buijs

Alice van Essen

Jolanda Dreijklufft

Julia Gorodecky

Allison Klein

Elise Reynolds

Ragini Werner

Tracy Brown Hamilton

Special thanks to Marjolijn Polman (International coordinator, *Flow* magazine)

front and back covers, pp. i, iii: illustrations, EurekartStudio.

pp. iv–v: illustration, Mevrouw Knot.

p. vi: illustration, Sarah Walsh.

pp. 1–3: text, Irene Smit and Astrid van der Hulst.

p. 2: illustration, Xuan Loc Xuan.

p. 3: illustration, Roeqiya Fris; photo, Danique van Kesteren.

Chapter 1:
LOVE YOUR ACTIVE BRAIN

pp. 4–5: text, Irene Smit and Astrid van der Hulst; illustration, Summer Candy/Adobe Stock.

pp. 6–9: text, Sara Madou; illustrations, Carolyn Gavin.

p. 10: photo, Alicia Bock.

Postcards: illustrations, Valesca van Waveren.

pp. 11–16: text, Caroline Buijs; illustrations, Karen Schipper.

pp. 17–19: text, Caroline Buijs; illustrations, We Are Out of Office (@wereoutofoffice).

pp. 20–22, 25: text, Sjoukje van de Kolk and Minke Tromp; hand-lettering, Valerie McKeehan.

p. 24: text, Sjoukje van de Kolk; illustration, Sylverarts Vectors/Shutterstock.

pp. 26–27: text, Fleur Baxmeier; illustrations, Hein Nouwens/Shutterstock.

Chapter 2:
LOVE YOUR IMPERFECT BODY

pp. 28–29: text, Irene Smit and Astrid van der Hulst; illustration, Summer Candy/Adobe Stock.

pp. 30–35: text, Otje van der Lelij; illustrations, Lucy Driscoll

pp. 36–40: text, Anneke Bots; illustrations, Xuan Loc Xuan; hand-lettering, Valesca van Waveren.

p. 42: text, Rachel Lancashire; illustrations, Valesca van Waveren.

Floral Fun Paper Flower: illustrations, Valesca van Waveren.

p. 43: text, Marie Hedderick Browne; illustration, Valesca van Waveren; paper, DW Labs Incorporated/Adobe Stock.

p. 44: photo, Miriam Bunse (@miricujaa); hand-lettering, Valerie McKeehan.

pp. 45–46: text, Sjoukje van de Kolk and Gary Ferguson.

p. 47: text, Leonard Cohen; photo, Lina Hamer.

pp. 48–50: text, Bernice Nikijuluw; photos, Anouk de Kleermaeker; styling, Anne-Marie Rem; hand-lettering, Valesca van Waveren.

pp. 52–53: text, Caroline Buijs; illustration, Kate Pugsley.

pp. 54–59: text, Hedwig Wiebes; illustrations, Karen Schipper; photos, Hedwig Wiebes.

p. 60: illustration, Mike Lowery.

p. 61: illustration, Karen Schipper; text, Irene Smit.

Chapter 3:
LOVE BEING ALONE

pp. 62–63: text, Irene Smit and Astrid van der Hulst; illustration, Summer Candy/Adobe Stock.

pp. 64–69: text, Caroline Buijs; illustrations, Yelena Bryksenkova.

pp. 70–73: text, Eva Loesberg; photos, Kyle Mims (@mimskyle).

p. 74: text, Rachel Lancashire; illustrations, Holly Maguire.

Bookmarks: illustrations, Holly Maguire, Sanny van Loon, Yelena Bryksenkova; text, Neil Gaiman, Haruki Murakami, Stephen King, and Nnedi Okorafor.

pp. 75–79: text, Annemiek Leclaire; illustrations, Lotte Dirks.

pp. 80–83: text, Carine de Kooning; photos, Vero/Stocksy.

pp. 84–85: text, Caroline Buijs; illustration, Ruby Taylor.

pp. 86–91: text, Ilse Savenije; illustrations, Lotte Dirks; photos, Ilse Savenije.

Chapter 4:
LOVE YOUR UNIQUE MIND

pp. 92–93: text, Irene Smit and Astrid van der Hulst; illustration, Nadezda Grapes/Adobe Stock.

pp. 94–99: text, Caroline Buijs; illustrations, Yinfan Huang.

ABOUT THE AUTHORS

IRENE SMIT and **ASTRID VAN DER HULST** are the founding creative directors of *Flow* magazine, an international publication packed with paper goodies and beautiful illustrations that celebrate creativity, imperfection, and life's little pleasures. Irene and Astrid began their magazine careers as editors at *Cosmopolitan* and *Marie Claire*. In 2008, inspired by their passion for paper and quest for mindfulness, they dreamed up the idea for their own magazine in a small attic. They are now the coauthors of more than twelve books and calendars including *A Book That Takes Its Time*, *The Tiny Book of Tiny Pleasures*, *The Big Book of Less*, and *My Perfectly Imperfect Life*. They each live with their families in Haarlem, the Netherlands. Visit flowmagazine.com to see more of their work.

ABOUT FLOW

FLOW is an international creative brand that celebrates slowing down, living consciously, and the pleasures of paper through books, magazines, and stationery. *Flow* magazine is a division of DPG Media B.V.